KU-648-570

FOR KRISTIEN

The Author is indebted to Eoin O'Mahony,
who once again gave generously of his
scholarship and of his intimate knowledge of
the family history of the period. Thanks are
also due to Columba McBride and Eva
Vosseler for assistance with the manuscript.

FOR KRISTIEN

. . . where to fail is more than to triumph,
And victory is less than defeat.

STEPHEN GWYNN.

LORD EDWARD FITZGERALD

CARTON, COUNTY KILDARE

LORD EDWARD FITZGERALD

Patrick Byrne

THE TALBOT PRESS LIMITED

EIGHTY-NINE TALBOT STREET, DUBLIN

FIRST PUBLISHED 1955

PRINTED IN THE REPUBLIC OF IRELAND BY THE TALBOT PRESS LTD.

Lord Edward Fitzgerald

◆

one

ON a summer afternoon in
the year 1534 the Council of Ireland was in session in
St. Mary's Abbey, Dublin. A dramatic scene took place
the accounts of which read like an excerpt from a Walter
Scott novel. A young man, aged twenty-one, dressed in
showy garments and followed by a troop of horse, rode
up and thundered at the Abbey doors. Being admitted,
he strode majestically to the Council table while the
assembly of elders and nobles kept silent, partly from
astonishment, partly from fear. Reaching the table, he
flung down the great Sword of State with a crash,
declaring that thus he severed his allegiance to King
Henry, accusing His Majesty, amongst other things, of
lechery, tyranny, and betrayal. The young man was no
less a person than Thomas Fitzgerald, Lord Offaly, the
acting King's Deputy in Ireland.

The Council witnessed this startling performance with
mixed feelings. There were quite a few present who
saw that their plans were working out as they expected:
they had led the young fool into this rash action by

spreading false rumours. For years there had been prayers for the downfall of the great Fitzgerald house, and now they saw that ruin and annihilation were on their way. But young Lord Offaly had a few friends there also. In particular there was the venerable and faithful Archbishop Cromer of Armagh, who besought him with tears in his eyes, to reconsider such rash actions. Offaly brushed him aside. We are told that at the psychological moment, when the entreaties of the Archbishop were making some impression, an old Irish harper in the retinue of Offaly struck up a martial air, and this, so to speak, was the last word. Offaly rode forth with his small band of followers proclaiming to the astonished citizens of Dublin that he, the acting Lord Deputy, was at war with the King.

It seems scarcely necessary to record the sequel. Offaly joined up with some of the Irish chiefs and maintained the war for a year. Then reinforcements arrived from England, the Fitzgerald stronghold at Maynooth was battered to pieces by the newly-introduced artillery, Offaly himself was hunted down and captured. Transported to London, he lingered miserably in cold and hunger in the Tower for a year. The eighth Henry, at the best of times was not noted for his merciful or humanitarian feelings, and it must be said that on this occasion he had received some provocation. The internal disputes of the nobles in Ireland seemed never-ending, and, rightly or wrongly, he blamed most of it on the Fitzgeralds. For a century they had ruled Ireland, each Fitzgerald being a kind of hereditary deputy for the King. Nevertheless, the retribution is horrifying—it was nothing other than the extermination of the family. The rebellion gave the King his opportunity. Offaly and his five uncles were beheaded, though two of them were innocent of any share in the rebellion; the great estates were confiscated and the blood was attainted. There w·s, it seemed, an end to the great House of Kildare, and for its enemies the triumph seemed complete. The line of the Geraldines, which for a hundred years had supplied the uncrowned kings of Ireland, was now wiped out save for a hunted youth of twelve years, Gerald, half-brother to Offaly, who was eagerly sought by the king's officers and harried from shelter to shelter in the remote provinces. Eventually he escaped to Italy and was reared in Florence.

This rebellion of Thomas Fitzgerald and its terrible sequel might be passed over as a normal event in the wild history of the times, but it had, in fact, a double significance. It marked the end of the earliest attempt at colonial home rule in Ireland. Henry promptly constituted himself King of Ireland, where hitherto he had exercised only a sort of feudal lordship. Though the Irish Parliament was retained, it was controlled from London, and so began that attempt, fraught with so much suffering, to govern Ireland from without. The second sequel has already been noted: the passing of the Kildares. The Fitzgeralds, originally a Florentine family named Gherardini, had come over with the Norman invasion of Ireland in the twelfth century. In time they branched into two main houses, the Desmonds, who were the feudal overlords in the South-West, and the Kildares, established in Leinster. Of the Desmonds it is sufficient for our purpose to say that, after many vicissitudes, they were finally extinguished during the reign of Elizabeth. It might seem that the Kildares had met with an even earlier fate, were it not that the young Gerald survived, and in Queen Mary's reign was recalled from Florence and restored to his title and the great Kildare estates in Leinster. But from the sixteenth century, the Kildares, once so powerful and a threat to English majesty itself, disappear from history. True, the Geraldine legend survived in folklore and ballad, the early Kildares had intermarried with the Irish and, without any great justification, had been held up as champions against the invader; even the Thomas Fitzgerald mentioned above has been passed down as a national hero. However, their allegiance changed, and henceforth when the Kildares appear at all it is always on the side of the English. The Earls married and prospered, they conformed to the Reformation, became great landowners and, so far as the troubled times would permit, for three hundred years they slumbered their lives away.

So we come to the eighteenth century. The political scene was not greatly changed, and Ireland was still governed—as the phrase went—in the English interest. The theory and trappings of an independent kingdom were maintained, but the realities were otherwise. For example there was a national Parliament which not only was unrepresentative but corrupt as well; there was an executive government which was not responsible to Parliament and took its orders as to policy from London. The constitutional development in Britain did not apply in Ireland: there was religious exclusion and there were unjust trading laws. This was a dangerous situation at a time when liberal ideas were growing; but those who governed in the British interest felt that they had nothing to fear. The native race—three-fourths of the population—was crushed and outlawed; the people were illiterate and were debased by poverty and penal-laws, nothing was to be feared from them. As for the others—the Anglo-Irish—it was clearly in their interest, being a privileged and small minority, to preserve things as they were and to foster the British connection.

In the early eighteenth century a new and unexpected, but definitely formidable, menace to the English interest appeared. The Anglo-Irish had developed ideas of what was afterwards called 'nationhood', and began to look on themselves as having certain rights distinct from those of England. As far back as Queen Anne's reign William Molyneux had published a book which he entitled *The Case for Ireland Stated*. We would not nowadays call it a very ' patriotic ' work, certainly not a subversive one—it was largely an argument about certain discriminations against Irish manufacturers—yet it so annoyed the Government that it was ordered to be burnt by the common hangman. Then the great name of Swift is linked with that of Molyneux as a pioneer. Swift was now consuming his disappointment in Dublin, where he spent over thirty miserable years. But the ' savage indignation ' with which Swift's reputation is associated, was, it should be noted, indignation within certain limits. In the face of a great mass of the injustice about him he was indifferent, or at least silent, but on those subjects towards which he directed his satire he caused great embarrassment. He propounded a colonial theory of self-sufficiency, he raised a small affair of monetary sharp practice to a historical importance by attacking it in a series of pamphlets, and he actually forced the administration to retreat. The Government was annoyed but not particularly worried. It was not until almost half-way through the eighteenth century that this type of opposition was carried within the portals of Parliament, and it came about in an unexpected way.

II

For the first half of the eighteenth century Ireland was in effect governed by a succession of three Church Primates, acting with others as Lords Justices for the absentee Lord Lieutenant. These men, Boulter, Hoadly, and Stone, were Archbishops, but they were nevertheless worldly-wise and, according to the standards of a rapacious economy, they were efficient. In the seventeen-forties the man in power was Primate Stone. He had many enemies, personal and otherwise.

Under the guidance of the successive Churchmen the central revenue had prospered, so that in the year 1753 there was a substantial surplus. This was unprecedented, and the question was what was to be done about it; a question which was obviously one for Parliament. Whatever other rights had been abdicated, however corrupt the assembly might be, English theory and usage had always insisted on parliamentary control of the funds. Long smouldering hates burst into flame, and a group formed themselves into something like an Opposition on the British model. They were called the ' Patriot Party ' in derision, for in England the term had fallen into such ill-odour that Johnson described Patriotism as ' The last refuge of a scoundrel '. Parliament showed some spirit, and refused to allow the money to be applied except by parliamentary consent. This seems elementary. But this insolence was not to be endured, and the action so provoked Stone and the Government that they thereupon filched the money out of the exchequer by a procedure known as a King's Letter.

The sequel was rather curious. In a first rush of indignation Stone declared a proscription and had everyone connected with the Opposition dismissed from Government office and patronage. Later the Government had reason to think better of the matter. To dismiss men from patronage and to penalise others was to give them all a personal grievance to add to a political enmity, and nothing cements an Opposition like personal resentments, nothing gives zest to political activity like the feeling that one is getting one's own back. The Government quickly saw that a blunder had been made, and Stone felt that, like the man with the evil spirit, his last state was worse than his first. Who could tell to what this parliamentary Opposition might lead?

There was one procedure open, rather humiliating it seems to us now, but one which the Government of the day regarded as a matter of course. The Government could bribe. They could confer office, give pensions and even make grants in cash. Where these were not effective they held out that bait to which eighteenth century gentlemen—and their wives—were particularly-susceptible, a peerage or a step in the peerage. The Opposition for the moment faded away, and the ranks of the peers of the realm were augmented by a body of newcomers.

Thus ended, rather ingloriously, the first sparkle of independence in the Parliament of the Kingdom of Ireland. It was nevertheless a turning point. Within a few years the Opposition revived, this time led by young men of genuine independence and spirit, and within twenty years the demands made transcended anything thought of hitherto, demands which might have made the Primate Stone turn pale with wrath.

III

In the year 1753 the 'Patriot' Opposition had an unexpected recruit when it was joined by a young man of illustrious family, bearing the title of twentieth Earl of Kildare. Of recent times the Kildares were un-distinguished, but the magic of the Geraldine name was still sufficient to reach out beyond the narrow political circles in Dublin. The young man had hitherto taken little interest in affairs but he had nevertheless a great dislike for the powerful Stone. To ventilate this he adopted an unusual course. He indited and sent across the Channel a Memorial, intended for the King himself, to which he gave the title of an ' Honest Remonstrance '. In this he set out what appeared to him to be the many faults and failings of the Primate. He took care to point out that he had nothing to ask of His Majesty for himself, neither place, civil or military, nor employment for himself or friends, and he laid stress on the loyalty of the Kildares to the Crown. Having made this clear, he enlarged on Stone, whom he describes as " a greedy Churchman, interesting himself with temporal power and affecting to be a second Wolsey in the State ". The ageing George II was not at all pleased with this curious document, but the Privy Council was not disturbed. They were accustomed to these complaints from Ireland, and like many subsequent British Governments, they had become a trifle bored by the Irish Question. Therefore they did not propose that any drastic action be taken. Stone, however, soon afterwards quitted the Irish Privy Council, though in effect he continued to hold power until his death, in 1764.

At home in Ireland the modern Wolsey sat glowering in his Castle of Leixlip, meditating appropriate revenge. Kildare he could not touch; he held no office and was a rich and popular landowner. But later, to the general disappointment, when overtures were made to the Opposition, and offices and titles were distributed, Kildare was included, and to him was held out the irresistible prize of a Dukedom. He, the twentieth Earl, was to be the premier Irish Duke, the first nobleman in the land, and accordingly in November 1766 he became Duke of Leinster.

two

I

IN 1744, a few years before
Kildare had penned his ' Honest Remonstrance ' against
Stone, there was a startling occurrence at Goodwood in
Sussex in the great household of the Duke of Richmond,
grandson of Charles II and Louise de Keroualle, Duchess
of Portsmouth. The Duke and his lady were beginning
to experience some worry about their marriageable
daughters. The eldest of these girls was not yet seventeen,
but all three, the ladies Caroline, Emily, and Georgiana,
were noted for their beauty and charm, and many suitors
were coming about the place. In the estimation of the
Duchess these could be divided approximately into two
classes, young men of noble family but with no money,
and young men with plenty of money but no family, and
her Ladyship could never quite decide which class she disliked the more. Then one night in 1744 the eldest, Lady
Caroline, climbed down from her window and eloped
with a certain Mr. Fox.

Mr. Fox's father, Sir Stephen Fox was a remarkable
man. Born as far back as 1627, his career stretched over
several troubled reigns, from that of Charles I to that of
George I. It was true that he had begun life as a retainer
of the Duke of Newcastle, but through that nobleman's
influence he made his way into Government circles, and

in the political changes of the times his achievement consisted chiefly in the successful maintenance of his equilibrium. He went abroad with the future Charles II and became a sort of public-relations officer for the exiled court. He seems to have had that knack of doing the right thing at the right time which is one of the secrets of success. For example in his capacity as intelligence officer he contrived somehow to obtain advance news of the death of Cromwell and was able to announce it six hours before the news reached anyone else. To have received the joyful news of the tyrant's death a full six hours before it reached the royalist coterie was a triumph never forgotten by Charles II, and Fox was a man marked out for favours at the Restoration. Eventually he became Paymaster-General and by some questionable management he died a millionaire. The diarist Evelyn, polite as always, said that he believed Fox got the money honestly, but, alas, no one else believed it. Be that as it may, it is necessary to mention one more achievement, and that by no means the least. Fox (by this time Sir Stephen) at the age of seventy-seven, finding himself without heirs for his wealth, married the buxom daughter of a country clergyman and had five children.

His son, who carried off Lady Caroline, was a brilliant and well-endowed politician, and was indeed soon to become a member of the Government; but it was rumoured that his father had started life as a valet. It was therefore presumptuous of young Mr. Fox to aspire to such a marriage as he did, and it was outrageous that Caroline should demean herself by falling in love with him. Sternly she had been forbidden to see him, and, though she married him, not for three years did the family consent to receive her and her young son. It remains to add that the marriage was a happy one. Mr. Fox was a kind and loving husband, he prospered well in the political field, was created Lord Holland, and for a number of years held the post of Paymaster-General. It seems needless to add that he died a millionaire. Holland House became an institution in English society, and his second son was the famous Charles James Fox.

The second daughter of Richmond was Lady Emily Lennox. She was a high-spirited girl, and after the dreadful Fox affair, the Duchess was determined not to be caught out again and was resolved to keep a close eye on her. She was an advanced young lady, for at the age of eleven she was already attending dances, and at thirteen she was writing seriously to her confidential girl-friend about male admirers. Among these was numbered a great Polish nobleman who dressed in beautiful silks and kept an equipage which astonished everyone in the Park. It was just at this time that the young Earl of Kildare came on the scene and the Polish gentleman was obliged to retire. Kildare was aged twenty-three and was a presentable young man, though a stylised portrait by Reynolds made later shows him to have had a rather sheep-like cast of features. He had made the Grand Tour, he was the first nobleman in Ireland, and he was not given to gambling or swearing. In fact in every way he was a most suitable match. Lady Emily herself, it must be admitted, writes about him to her friend without enthusiasm ; but the family was favourably inclined, and they were married in London in February 1747, Emily Lennox being aged fifteen years and a few months. Their first child, a boy, was born the following January.

II

Kildare went back to Ireland and busied himself with his estate, particularly with the restoration of his country seat, Carton, in County Kildare, and the building of

B

the great new town mansion, Kildare House (afterwards Leinster House) in Molesworth Fields a hitherto unfashionable part of the town. He began to dabble in politics, and, as we have seen was soon involved in the quarrel with Primate Stone. Later in life Kildare took no great part in politics. He received his dukedom and lived to enjoy his title for only seven years, but his popularity was such that he was known, at least in early life, as the " beloved Kildare ".

Although indolent in political affairs the Duke, judged even by eighteenth century standards, was in no way neglectful of his marital duties. His girl-wife bore her first child when she was just over sixteen. Thenceforward at yearly intervals her children arrived regularly, nineteen in all, spaced over a married life of twenty five years. And she seemed to enjoy the experience, so much so that, as we shall see, within a year of the Duke's death, and being then aged forty-two, she was eager to begin again.

James, the first Duke, died in 1773, but some years previously there was introduced into the household a man who was to influence the widowed Emily's future. He was William Ogilvie who was employed as tutor for the young boys. Ogilvie was a Scotsman who came to Dublin as a school-usher, and that business having failed he was glad of this new employment. We do not know very much about his earlier years though he himself claimed to be related to distinguished Scottish families. His personal appearance was not an asset, certainly it did not please the rather spiteful women of Dublin, for he is described as tall and lanky, scowling and ugly, and to the end of his days he had a broad Scottish accent. Of scholarship he possessed sufficient to act as an efficient and kindly tutor to the boys but there is no evidence that he possessed any more.

So much, on the debit side, is not reassuring, but out of this some contradictions emerge. The first is that in a

to be placated. Emily herself wrote to the Duke of Richmond, her brother, whose own amours, as befitted a great-grandson of Charles II, disposed him to be generous. In fact he placed his great house at Aubigny, in the province of Berri, at the disposal of the Duchess and her family, and Emily moved there in 1776. Here life was pleasant and uneventful. The house was well situated, surrounded by woods and lawns, but the place was hot in summer, and the great rooms were hard to heat in winter. Emily had grown tired of the endless social round in England and Ireland, she had no regrets for the loss of her status as the first Peeress in Ireland, and on the whole she was quite content. She varied the calm by trips to Paris where she complained that the noise and traffic kept her awake at nights, and the gossip and trivialities of the salons got on her nerves. She was always glad to return to Aubigny, to join in the laughter of her children, and to enjoy her gentle walks around the park in the cool of the evening accompanied by Ogilvie.

The twelfth child and fifth son of the first Duke of Leinster and Lady Emily Lennox was Lord Edward Fitzgerald, who was born in London on 15th October, 1763. He spent his formative years in the tranquil surroundings of Aubigny. He was only twelve when the family went there, and some two or three years later he, with his brother Henry, attended an academy in Paris, but most of the time was spent in the country. These were happy years. The family was a large and friendly one, and there were two little Ogilvie girls whom everyone loved. Mr. Ogilvie was a dutiful step-father, and, remembering his former vocation, he now took the education of the children in hand, varying this occupation with trips to England or Ireland, which journeys he always described, rather oddly, as a quest for employment.

III

Even in those early days Lord Edward felt the impulse to an active military career ; he could not think of any calling save that of a soldier. His ideas were not those of a drawing-room officer, resplendent in uniform and attractive to the ladies. He wanted the real thing. He longed for service and danger, for adventure overseas, and he was not troubled by any speculation as to the brutality of war or the causes for which he would fight. He desired fighting for its own sake, as a noble facet of the the manly life. At this early age he was impatient to be off, anxious to go across the seas to seek out hazard and peril ; and so powerful was the feeling that neither the affections of family life nor love for his mother could stand in the way. Ogilvie therefore directed the studies of the fourteen year-old boy along military lines. He read books about camps and fortifications, route-marches and strategy. He studied the conventional accounts of the campaigns of great captains like Alexander and Caesar, as well as the histories of the more recent religious wars. Lord Edward skipped the parts dealing with politics and patriotism, as he was eager to get on to the details of the battles. He was a fairly diligent student. He surveyed the neighbourhood and con- structed plans for camps and fortifications according to the latest scientific ideas. He was highly satisfied with his own work. There appears to be some justification for this feeling, for when shortly afterwards he was posted in a militia battalion in England he was able to teach some of the regular officers their business; a proceeding which may not have added to his popularity.

His way in the world was not a steep ascent. He was the brother of Leinster and the nephew of Richmond and he was assured of a reasonably ample income whatever happened. In 1779 the whole Fitzgerald family removed from France to England owing to the trouble between the two countries. Uncle Richmond was colonel of the Sussex militia and Edward, then sixteen, got an appointment in the militia; a year later he secured a lieutenancy in a foot regiment—the 96th—stationed at the time in Ireland, but waiting for orders to proceed to America. The seventeen-year old lieutenant accordingly joined his regiment at Youghal, Co. Cork and here he had his first experience of the realities of military life. He was fortunate that, unlike so many youthful enthusiasts, he found everything up to expectations; and his first care, as always, was to write delightedly to his mother.

Youghal was in great excitement at the arrival of the regiment and the young ladies of the neighbourhood, true to the tradition of Jane Austen, were " in a great hurry " (as Fitzgerald rather ungallantly put it) " to show themselves off to the officers ". There were many assemblies and Fitzgerald entered with zest into this pleasant and unexpected side of army life. He wrote to Ogilvie a characteristic letter, thanking him for his careful tuition and assuring him that all his own principles and sentiments were due to Ogilvie, and that he hoped to repay the debt by his affection. Meantime the winter in Co. Cork wore on and, as was natural, the brother of Leinster had many invitations to stay with the gentry in the neighbourhood. He spent happy days at Lord Shannon's seat at Castle Martyr—Shannon who as Mr. Speaker Boyle had been Kildare's associate in the Patriots but who was also bought off with a title. It was here that he met an old family acquaintance, Lady Inchiquin, who must have been a family celebrity, for Lord Edward notes that " she is still wearing the same maroon-coloured dress that she wore before the Fitzgeralds left Ireland, only now it is made up differently." Here also he met a Miss Sandford whose only interest for us now is that

Fitzgerald shows by his appraisement of her that already he had a discerning eye for the ladies, and also that not even the possibilities of love-making combined with affection for his mother could interfere with his impatience to depart to the wars.

As the Spring days passed by the danger seemed to be that the half-hearted war in America would be over and done with before Fitzgerald could strike a blow for the maintenance of kingly stupidity and autocracy against the colonists. He was anxious for promotion, to get a company of his own and to be a captain or even a major ; he wrote discreetly about this to Ogilvie, reminding him that Richmond had the ear of the Prime Minister, or possibly even of the King himself ; but he points out that if promotion meant missing the war then promotion would have to wait. He began to worry that the representations in high quarters might after all have effect, and that he might be promoted captain and transferred elsewhere. His fear and impatience grew as the days passed. At last relief came. The transports put in to Cork harbour, and at the end of March they set sail. As the ship fared westward it bore him to a comparatively unknown land, inhabited, so it was said, by savages and a few misguided and disloyal colonists. There he was to encounter danger, excitement, the possibility of an obscure and painful death. There he was to fight in a struggle, the merits of which he had not considered—he was a soldier and he must obey orders and the ethics of the matter were simplified accordingly. This much however he did know, and it worried him. His cousin Charles James Fox opposed the war warmly, so did other men for whose intellectual quality he had an equal respect, while for long he had considered Lord North, the Prime Minister, an obstinate old blunderer. But such troubles faded momentarily from mind as in the blaze of June sunshine the transports sailed into Charleston.

IV

Actually the war was nearly over but the arrival of these reinforcements from Ireland altered the situation for a short time, at least in the limited districts in which they operated in Carolina. Lord Rawdon was in command at Charleston and his immediate concern was to succour General Greene at a fort called ' Ninety Six '. This he was now enabled to do and even to extend his operations further. It was said that the American commanders were intimidated by the news that new troops " full of ardour " had arrived.

One of them at least was full of ardour, but the question was how was the zeal to be expended in a war which was unpopular and which in any case was nearly lost ? Fitzgerald resolved that he would, as it were, have to do something desperate. He did succeed, in a brave rearguard action, in covering the retreat of his regiment, and for this exploit he received what may have seemed to him doubtful promotion, namely appointment on Lord Rawdon's staff. Staff-officers are not necessarily fighters. Lord Edward may have had visions of himself mouldering away at headquarters, checking dispatches and retailing gossip to the General. He was assured however that this was a great chance to learn the art of war under an experienced officer on an active front, and in those days Generals and their staffs were not altogether office-men. They frequently made a sally into active combat and the young staff-officer could therefore hope for the best. Soon however Rawdon was recalled to England and Fitzgerald rejoined his regiment on the active front.

In the Autumn the war took a more serious turn in this sector and an engagement which exactly suited his temperament resulted. This is sometimes referred to as the battle of Eubaw Springs. It was a savage, almost hand-to-hand encounter between evenly matched forces and the result was a draw. The officers as well as the men fought hand-to-hand. Fitzgerald, with his usual recklessness, was foremost in the fight and inevietably was severely wounded. He received a leg injury which was so serious that he was left for dead on the field. When the fight was over he was found by a poor negro squatter who carried him off to his own hut and nursed him until he was removed to Charleston. This negro was the faithful Tony whom Lord Edward adopted as his body-servant and who remained with him to the end.

Soon afterwards Cornwallis surrendered at Yorktown and the American war was ended. The British troops in Carolina were transferred to St. Lucia in the West Indies and here Lord Edward got a comfortable job on the staff of General O'Hara. His American career was short but not altogether inglorious. He thirsted for active service, that is to say mass slaughter, and he found it ; several times he was in immediate danger of death and he was in fact severely wounded. It may well puzzle us that this boy of twenty to whom the world offered so much could deem life of so little account.

V

St. Lucia in the early springtime could be a pleasant enough place, but Fitzgerald very soon grew restless ; he wanted to see the world, but he also wished that things would keep on happening. Nothing could ever happen in St. Lucia, so he consoled himself by making a study of the fortifications, and noted in a letter to his mother that these were deplorable although the English had been there for four years. He was fortunate too in that the general in command of the Barbadoes was O'Hara, who, he said, reminded him of Ogilvie for the doubtful reason that he did not trust others and always insisted on doing things himself.

There were other variations in the routine. He went under a flag of truce on a visit to Martinique and there found that things were much more lively. The women were gay and pretty and in a meaning phrase he described them as " good-natured ", which he explains cautiously was the term used by the French officers. He went to a ball every night and stayed altogether a week. A new worry now loomed on the horizon. England was still at war both with France and Spain, but everyone was talking about peace. Peace, indeed, had already been concluded with the Americans and Lord Edward, as it were, saw the bottom falling out of his world. Suddenly the glad news came that there would be no peace with France or Spain, but one could not be sure, and Fitzgerald writes to his mother that they were anxious to have some confirmation of this news, as the peace, he says, " frightens everybody ".

In these unsettled circumstances his thoughts turned to projects which the excitement of action had obscured, the most important, as always, was his chance of promotion. He was twenty-one, he had four years service and he considered that at least he should be given a company of the Guards. That was the great objective. So he wrote to his mother and suggested that she and her connections might reasonably exert themselves ; others had got similar promotion, there was no reason why he should not get it also. Meantime he held in reserve an alternative suggestion and one almost equally appealing. The war, he believed, would be shifted to the Far East and Cornwallis might be sent in command there. The more he pondered the war in the east, the more attractive it seemed and his hopes in this theatre were for nothing less than a lieutenant-colonelcy.

1657

He got neither one nor the other. Instead the sojourn in the West Indies petered out in boredom and petty annoyances. He got letters from the agent at home about his property in Co. Kildare and these worried him, until in the end instead of fearing peace he began to wish he could return to Ireland. The representations to obtain a company of Guards, if made at all, had not prospered and there is something unexplained in the fact that such powerful friends (with Richmond actually a Minister) could not procure this small place. As subsequent tragic events show there was a strong family feeling amongst the Richmonds and the Fitzgeralds, yet Richmond on this occasion made the plea recognisable as the stock excuse of persons in power. He said that he did not like asking favours for friends. Lord Edward, annoyed, countered with an ingenious bit of sophistry. He said Richmond was wrong in stating that he did not like to ask a favour, because as Minister he does not ' ask ' a favour, the thing being in the gift of the Ministry. He was perhaps trying to draw a distinction between the Ministry and the ' Crown ', a division never very clear in British theory and one of little consolation to disappointed place-seekers.

It was now clear that he was wasting time in the West Indies. He had been two years abroad which he reckoned as two years absence from his mother. The desire to see her again grew stronger and stronger ; there was nothing now to detain him. So he paid another pleasant week-long visit to Martinique where doubtless he enjoyed the the favours of those good-natured dark-eyed West Indian girls, and in the summer of 1783 he set sail for Ireland.

three

I

THE interpretation of modern Irish history usually proceeds on the assumption that Ireland was a conquered and subject state. This assumption, it may be said, is not entirely accurate. But it is important to note that the doctrine of the responsibility of the Executive to Parliament, which is inherent in the British Constitution was not effective in Ireland. As a result the British Cabinet, despite the independence laws of 1782 and 1783 maintained an unwarranted interference in Irish affairs and had in effect the last word on policy. This interference was deemed ' the source of all our evils '.

The United Irishmen movement, which will figure largely in the narrative to follow, was at first, neither republican nor separatist. The rebellion of 1798 was not, as is often claimed, an assertion in arms by the Irish people of their nationhood and independence. It was in essence a civil war, partly a democratic rising aiming at universal suffrage and reform, partly a Catholic revolt directed against tithes and landlords. Not until near the end were British troops called in. It is often overlooked that the evil laws by which Ireland was governed in the latter half of the eighteenth century were the work of Irishmen sitting in Dublin and that it was an accident of

history that England had a hand in the game. If the
Foxite Whigs had come into power conditions would
have been far otherwise ; interference by the British
cabinet was a Tory policy undertaken in concert with the
Tory class in Dublin.

Ireland was then, in 1783, in constitutional theory
at least, an independent state. Parliamentary independence resulted from a conjunction of three separate events,
the defeat of England in the American war, the advent to
power of a Whig administration in England, and the
resolutions passed at the Volunteer Convention in
Dungannon, Co. Tyrone. These Volunteers had been
organised in 1775 to resist a possible French invasion and
were a citizen force, loyal and for the main part Protestant.
There was a threat of a European coalition against
Britain, and in her dark hour the British Government was
in no mood to dispute claims by the Irish, backed as they
were by the armed Volunteers. The lesson of the American war was very recent.

The King, Lords and Commons of Ireland were now
therefore the sole law-making authority, and the association with England was preserved by the slender link of
a common monarch. So much for appearances. But
this legislature suffered from almost every defect that it is
possible to conceive.

Firstly it was hopelessly unrepresentative ; it was
simply a haphazard collection of individuals drawn from
a narrow class and determined at whatever cost to
preserve the privileges of that class. There were, it is
true, sixty-four members, two for each county, elected
by ' forty-shilling free-holders '; but voting was open
and Catholics were altogether excluded from the franchise. And what were sixty-two in an assembly of three
hundred ? For the rest they were all returned to Parliament by single patrons or by boroughs with a few electors.
Those members returned by patrons either purchased

their place, a transaction deemed normal and quite in course, or else they were returned by the patron pledged to support his policy; while the Government controlled sufficient boroughs to ensure a perpetual majority. The Lords sat by hereditary right.

The second defect was that there was no clearly defined and responsible Executive. The Government at this time consisted of the Lord Lieutenant (the King's Deputy) and an Irish Privy Council. The Lord Lieutenant, invariably an Englishman, was nominally the representative of the King, but in reality was a creature of the British Cabinet and took his policy from Downing Street. He ruled through the Irish Privy Council and certain Office holders forming a sort of Cabinet. Parliamentary control was non-existent, even on such a fundamental matter as supply, because the Government by bribery and manipulation could rely on a majority in Parliament. Nor, in the event of defeat in the Commons was there a change of Government.

The third and greatest defect was that undefined thing already referred to known as the ' English connection '. What was this ? To understand it is to appreciate the whole tragic story of the times.

The population of Ireland was three-fourths Catholic and Gaelic—outside Ulster the proportion was even higher. Whatever the theory, these Catholic people looked on themselves as a conquered race awaiting the day of resurgence ; they deemed England to be the aggressor and the Dublin Government merely an instrument to preserve that domination. The ballads made by the wandering Gaelic poets of the eighteenth century show that such was the attitude, though a century and a half of degradation had rendered the peasantry illiterate and inarticulate. The poets, like the ancient Hebrew poets, sang always of a time when their dear land would once again come into its own, and their imagery was a cloudy blending of a Stuart restoration and a return of the ancient Gaelic kings. In practice the Catholic people were politically ineffectual, they had developed a cringing and degenerate attitude, the result of outlawry and the Penal laws, and traces of this subservience are to be found even to-day. As for the middle and upper-class Catholics, they displayed a fawning and effusive loyalty, which not only disgusted the Presbyterians in their own day, and was secretly despised by such men as Fitzgibbon, but has caused subsequent generations of Irishmen to feel ashamed.

It was obvious that this people had an overwhelming political strength, yet they were held in subjection by a small class of Anglo-Irish, chiefly land-owners. It was a struggle which never ceased, one which required an ' eternal vigilance '. The privilege of the Anglo-Irish could not be maintained by inherent power for there were liberal ideas about, and even English Tories were worried some-times about the regime in Ireland. At any moment the explosion might come, and the French, while propound-ing a pernicious doctrine termed ' democracy ', were call-ing on all subject peoples to rise.

The privilege of a small minority became known later as ' Protestant Ascendancy ', and the urgent question was how it was to be maintained in view of the growth of liberal ideas. The answer was a simple one —preserve the connection with England. This connection is not easy to define but it meant in a last analysis the use of the coercive power of British arms to preserve the Irish junta in power, for British troops could always be imported under Parliamentary sanction by the Irish Executive.

It may be suspected that British statesmen were not too pleased with this arrangement. True, they wished to preserve an Irish connection of some sort, for the strat-egic importance of the adjacent island, then as later, was of supreme importance. But the Whig politicians were often uneasy at the price to be paid in conscience. They could not appreciate the argument that a connection could be preserved only by the domination by a narrow class of place-holders and landlords, and by invoking principles which outraged every liberal sentiment of the British constitution. But for the reactionary Government in power as a result of the French wars, this Whig feeling would have prevailed, The Irish Parliament would have been reformed, and reform, even on a mild scale would have swept away for ever the regime of the ascendancy.

II

It was at this juncture that a remarkable man named John Fitzgibbon, afterwards Lord Chancellor with the title of Earl of Clare, came to the forefront in Irish affairs. Fitzgibbon's grandparents were Catholic peasants in the county Limerick; his grandmother had a local renown as a singer of Gaelic folk-songs. The Earl's father, also named John, was a runaway clerical-student who turned Protestant and was called to the Bar. His subsequent career is obscure, he lived quietly in a Dublin suburb, making what seemed an adequate living as a practising Barrister. But there is some mystery about him, for when he died he was able to leave his son, the future Chancellor, an estate worth £5,000 a year. John the son, was born in 1748 and was also admitted to the Bar. Whether from heredity or for some pathological reason, he developed a fanatical hatred of Catholics remarkable even in those days.

Fitzgibbon's chief purpose in life therefore was to preserve the ascendancy, and in what he now saw as a desperate situation he would have no truck with sentiment or liberalism. He was, as we would say nowadays, a realist. His attitude was simple and direct, he would ask his fellow-members in Parliament : " Do you, or do

c

you not, wish to preserve the ascendancy, that is to say your lands and rents and the vast patronage of the national revenue for your hangers-on ? If you do you had better realise that you are in a beleaguered fortress."

In reading the speeches and memoranda of Fitzgibbon one cannot withhold admiration for his courage. He has been described as a man without any abstract sense of justice. The world in which he lived, or at least the regime which he sought to maintain, did not derive its stability from principles of justice ; he had the grace to admit this frankly and his policy seemed logical. The Catholic religion he did not hate as such—indeed, like many politicians of his age, he had developed an impatience with all organised religion—but he held that it was imperative to preserve the bogey of the Catholic danger to bolster up a non-representative Parliament. He was impatient of the dull and rather stupid following upon which the Castle depended for support in Parliament. Sometimes it was difficult to rely on this following, so he developed a technique of letting loose a shaft which he knew would strike home. Thus on one occasion he reminded them in a few terse sentences that the tenure of their lands derived from comparatively recent confiscations and was legalised only by statutes of the Irish Parliament ; if, he argued, you admit the rabble to Parliament, what will become of these tenures ?

It was one thing for Fitzgibbon to deal with the Irish but it was sometimes quite a different problem to persuade the English. English cabinet ministers—Dundas for example—were never quite at ease with the way things were going in Ireland. The responsibility was not entirely theirs, it is true, but it is equally true that the Castle rule could not be maintained except by this ill-defined connection with England. The British statesmen were not always deceived by the profession of ' loyalty ', and they worried at times as to why the prestige of England, the home of free men, should be used to sustain abuses which were crying out for remedy. And in any event, if it was loyalty that was at stake, did not the Catholics themselves outdo the junta in protestations of affection for His Majesty ? And were not the Bishops forever thundering denunciations of democracy and liberalism, and all the other doctrines of the French Revolution ?

It was not always easy to meet these objections and even Mr. Pitt himself was in a dilemma. For at least two reasons he wished to preserve the ' connection '—he sympathised, however covertly, with his Tory friends in Ireland, and was anxious to see preserved to them their wealth and privilege, and secondly he appreciated the strategic position of Ireland in time of war. On the other hand, beset by a half-wit king and with a French war on his hands, he, like so many subsequent English statesmen, became tired of the Irish question. Why could it not be settled finally and satisfactorily ? He suggested as a start that there should be some form of Catholic emancipation, but it was speedily pointed out that ' emancipation ' in Ireland was a very different matter from a similar action in England, where the Catholics were an insignificant minority.

We do not know what secret bargains were made, what private memoranda were exchanged, or what confidential conversations took place in the seventeen-nineties. One thing is certain, the Castle junta had the ear of powerful and reactionary friends in England. One has but to consider the steps taken by Beresford and his clique when they were swept from office during the Fitzwilliam episode. Beresford did not waste time in Dublin, instead he took ship to England and there paid a round of visits to his prominent Tory friends. The result was immediate and decisive.

III

By 1790 it was becoming clear to the Irish Government that the admission of Catholics to the full franchise could not be indefinitely delayed. Pitt was now posing as the ally of the Pope and the Catholic sovereigns abroad against the French, and it was absurd that at the same time His Majesty's Catholic subjects at home should suffer persecution. Fitzgibbon did not fear the granting of the vote, provided only that the franchise remained as it was. Obviously what was really to be feared was a combination of the franchise and reform ; this at the moment seemed inevitable and then all would be lost.

In this desperate strait Fitzgibbon hit on a brilliant idea. George III for long had been half-crazy, and was eventually to become completely mad. In his more lucid moments the King was noted for that most difficult type of obstinacy, namely that which springs from good intentions. To this monarch, Fitzgibbon managed to convey direct, by way of memorandum, the subtle hint that any pandering to Catholics would be a violation of his coronation oath, for was he not sworn to maintain the Protestant religion as by law established ? To the half-mad monarch, this suggestion, associated with oaths and high principles, had a certain nightmare intensity. In agitation he sent for Mr. Pitt. Pitt was perturbed at this new development, but he had other serious preoccupations. He had therefore no desire for a dynastic crisis, for at the time of George's bickerings with Lord North, the king always held in reserve the curious threat of " taking ship to Hanover " ; indeed this phantom ship—like that of the Flying Dutchman—hovered for a quarter century in the background of British politics. Pitt undertook that for the moment nothing more would be said about admitting Catholics to Parliament and Fitz-gibbon was satisfied that the kind of reform which would be effective in Ireland was staved off during the lifetime—or at least the sanity—of the King.

The causes of Irish unrest were indeed deep and varied. On the one hand there were the poetic visions of ballad-makers and on the other there was the democracy of the Ulster Presbyterians, which was inspired by and related to the Presbyterian faith. The Presbyterians represented the finest political type in eighteenth-century Ireland. They had no great love for the papists ; indeed not without reason, they frequently despised them ; but they believed above all in tolerance and humanity, and they threw up leaders remarkable for nobility and un-selfishness. The names of Orr, McCracken and Monroe are deeply reverenced throughout Ireland. Clearly an alliance between those competent northern folk and the Catholic Irish, remarkable for their endurance and physical bravery, would prove truly formidable.

four

I

SUCH was the position when Lord Edward returned to Ireland in 1783. Things had quietened down in the West Indies and for the present his prospects of promotion were at an end ; Richmond was unwilling to exert himself and there was in consequence nothing to be done. He grew tired of a tame war. He had recovered from the wound in his thigh but he considered himself a disappointed and ill-used man.

Yet to a modern wage-earner Lord Edward's station and prospects must seem extraordinarily alluring. Even his appearance and personality were favourable. He was a young man in the early twenties, of medium height, not stoutly built, with thick dark hair brushed low over the temples. His face was rounded but the features were regular and open. The expression, if not intellectual was kindly. His eyes were merry and could lend animation and he radiated great charm. It is rare to find a historical figure about whom there is such unanimity as to kindliness and sincerity. He was deferential to all men, great and humble alike, and he was beloved by all ; even his bitterest political enemies—some of them men without scruples—could scarce find words to praise his goodness, and not a single unfavourable comment is recorded. Again, the record of his affection for his mother reads like an idyll; at the age of ten he was already the favourite son. In all the distractions of battle or politics his thoughts turned towards her, and as the letters show, there was nothing sentimental or morbid in this affection. Indeed these letters, which have been preserved, are one of the most remarkable collections in the language. They are sincere and unaffected, but in the descriptions of scenery and reflections on life there is evidence of thought and literary grace.

His material prospects were favourable. He was the son of the premier Irish Duke and the nephew of a powerful English Duke. He was the cousin of Fox, the leading English statesman in the Opposition, and in one way or another he was connected with half a dozen great families. He was a younger son and according to the standards of eighteenth-century matrons, Edward Fitzgerald would not be rich. Yet he was well endowed, for in the family settlement he held a small estate at Kilrush in the County Kildare and his income was about £800 a year, equal at least to four times that figure in present day currency, and free of income tax as well.

There is no evidence that at this stage he had any views on Irish political questions. He had spent much of his childhood abroad and he now looked upon residence in Ireland as a dull interlude in a career of military glory. But his sympathies were already with the Whigs and he had a great admiration for Charles James Fox. He had no regular education in the sense of school and university, but very early in life he developed a taste for quiet and serious reading, remarkable in a young man whose interests lay otherwise in a military life. Besides, under the generous guidance of Ogilvie he received a grounding in essentials and he had read widely in military textbooks. At no period of his short career was Lord Edward credited with intellectual attainments, yet we are reminded that he read Rousseau with interest while stationed in the Canadian backwoods, and the mere fact that he could transcend environment and upbringing and align himself with revolution shows vigour and independence of mind. Only men endowed with unusual mental energy are capable of discarding the beliefs implanted in childhood and sanctified by custom, and which come therefore to be regarded as immutable truths. Lord Edward was one of these rare individuals.

In 1783 Edward Fitzgerald found himself a member of the Irish Parliament, nominated by his brother Leinster for the family borough of Athy. The young member found the political and social climate of Dublin unbearable. This is surprising, since, with new-found Parliamentary independence, political agitation was active and the session of Parliament which commenced in October was sufficiently theatrical to satisfy even an impatient young subaltern. In Parliament, Lord Edward's leader was Henry Grattan, the hero of the hour; he was the man who had secured legislative independence; he was now to address himself to the great question of reform.

Grattan, by profession a lawyer, was at heart a liberal politician, but he had the intellectual limitations of his class. His benevolence was aristocratic and he was not in advance of his time. He believed democracy to be a French invention which would bring evil on society and his view was that the elective franchise should be given to those only who, in his own words, " are likely to exercise it for the public good." We must not be too hard on him for this : " Law " wrote Jonathan Swift " in a free Country is, or ought to be the Determination of the Majority of those who have Property in Land." And over a hundred years later the urbane and scholarly Lecky could declare that to introduce a broad franchise would take the government of the country out of the hands of

the responsible gentlemen of property and hand it over
to a collection of Land Leaguers, rebels and political
adventurers. He was right, but the results were not so
disastrous as he expected. It is true that Grattan
believed in reform, but not on reform ' based on the
people's will '. Within these limitations he was a strong
champion of the franchise for Catholics, realising that
the Catholic political view was essentially aristocratic
and he even advocated that Catholics be admitted to
sit in Parliament. He considered, perhaps correctly,
that the religious intransigeance of Irish Catholics was
political, and that so soon as repression was removed,
the Catholics would all eventually become Protestants ;
the best method of killing religious enthusiasm being
to tolerate all religions.

The other popular leader was Henry Flood, who was
a different type from Grattan. Intellectually he was
better endowed and he possessed a greater sweep of
vision. Though loyal to the British Crown, Flood was
not altogether colonial in his views. For one thing he
linked up the present independence of the Kingdom of
Ireland with the old Gaelic state, a rare sequence of
thought in those days. He even studied the Irish language
and had some knowledge of Gaelic poetry. His reform
schemes went much further than those of Grattan and
approximated to the universal suffrage of the French
Revolution ; but against that he was opposed to full
enfranchisement of the Catholics. This was an attitude
which he seems to have found difficult to explain even to
himself. He was not intolerant of religion, and he may
truly be said to have been a democrat ; still his final
attitude was evasive, an uneasy argument that—for the
moment at any rate—emancipation of Catholics was
inexpedient.

The session, as expected, proceeded forthwith to a
discussion of reform, but the debate degenerated into a

violent private quarrel between Grattan and Flood. Grattan's personal position was vulnerable because he had once accepted £50,000 from Parliament for his services in securing independence, while on the other hand Flood had once accepted office, and had supported the sending of Irish troops to fight against the colonists in America. Personal gibes of a damaging kind could therefore be flung at both. There were high scenes in the House, and the inevitable challenge to a duel, which however (after both men had made their wills) ended in fiasco, as the sheriffs were on the ground when they arrived, and arrested them both. They were never afterwards on friendly terms.

But the chief public interest was centred outside Parliament, on a convention of the Volunteers held in the great hall of the Rotunda. The Volunteers were fond of conventions. In an age which loved the pomp of assembly, and when even ladies delighted to listen to long speeches, these conventions suited the public taste. They had the additional advantage that delegates must wear their uniforms and there was an excuse for a magnificent display of green and gold. But the conventions also had their serious side. It was the assembly in Dungannon in 1778 that led directly to the independence of Parliament and a further gathering had taken place in the same town which caused the Government much worry. At a subsequent date a Catholic convention gave the Castle junta such a fright that they proclaimed it as illegal and then procured a law declaring all conventions illegal—a law which half a century later was to prove an embarrassment to Daniel O'Connell.

The present Volunteer convention was the most daring of all to date, for, while Parliament was actually sitting, it constituted itself a sort of rival assembly in a nearby hall, and proceeded, as Fitzgibbon phrased it, " to probe and explore the Constitution with a bayonet ".

It had the advantage that it could claim to be at least as representative as Parliament itself. Like nearly all assemblies of this type it could afford to proclaim loudly that it was loyal and law-abiding, that it merely had the deep interests of the nation at heart. After these noble protests it is sad to reflect that its end was an anti-climax.

The convention sitting in the Rotunda, after much debate, framed certain resolutions for the reform of Parliament. On a Saturday afternoon when the resolution was passed, it was arranged that Henry Flood himself should then and there go to the neighbouring building in College Green where Parliament was in session and ask leave to present a motion. Flood departed and the delegates stayed on to hear the result. The evening wore on, night fell, and still the emissary did not return. The weary delegates at length went home— after midnight.

Meantime Henry Flood arrived on the floor of the Commons in the vivid uniform of the Volunteers and presented his motion. The House very promptly threw it out. It was clear now that the whole manoeuvre was ill-designed ; it was indeed a tactical error of the first magnitude. The Parliament, corrupt and unrepresentative as it was, could pose as the legitimate legislative body according to the Constitution, and could claim to be defending Parliamentary rule against the threat of coercion by armed men. The incident is of importance as it marked the end of the influence of the Volunteers. They lingered on for some years, but they were now without a united purpose; the more moderate grew tired of play-acting in uniform, but a section drifted into a new organisation which was destined to carry on the tradition of armed resistance. After the outbreak of the French war in 1792 the Volunteers were supressed by law.

II

Such was the outstanding event of Lord Edward's
first session in Parliament. In all, at this time, he spent
about three years in Ireland and it was his first real experience of the country. As a member of Parliament and
a leading figure in the younger Dublin aristocratic set he
went into society and in those days the Dublin season,
during the residence of the Viceroy was equal to the
London season in brilliance. All the great landlords
had their town mansions, and the lesser gentry had
houses in those stately Georgian streets and squares
which date from this period, and are even now the glory
of Dublin. Nonetheless, Lord Edward, who hated
class pretensions, found the ennui extreme. In August
he wrote to his mother from his brother's seat, Carton,
where he was staying : " Really a man must be a clever
fellow who after being a week at Carton and seeing nobody but Mr. and Mrs. B. can write a letter. If you
insist on letters I must write you an account of my American campaigns over again, as that is the only thing I
can remember. I am just now interrupted by the horrid
parson ; and he can find nothing to do but sit at my
elbow ".

But these were happy if uneventful years. Ogilvie and
the Duchess were in the villa at Blackrock, after an
absence of six years. On the outbreak of war in 1779
between England and France they decided to leave the
continent ; and with those of the family who still lived
with them they had returned to Ireland. ' Frescati ', the
villa, stood on an eminence exposed to the north and
east winds, but had magnificent views northward across
the bay and southward along the valley with the
mountains in the distance. Edward came to love this
place with a love which never left him. For the moment

indeed, apart from the cessation of his military career, one would think that he had most things in life to make him happy. He was united with his mother, living in the same house with her, and to the young soldier of twenty-two to whom the exclusive drawing-rooms and assemblies of Dublin were open, this was the highest bliss. He was well connected with the families of the larger country houses near Dublin and spent much time in visits. What his feelings were on these visits is not recorded. Did he observe the misery of the peasants, living on small holdings outside the demesne walls and paying great rents to keep these palatial homes in existence? Or did he note the squalor of the Dublin slums?

He visited London in 1784, and was active as a canvasser for the Whigs in the general election of that year. This is interesting as a definate indication of political views. He was much influenced by his cousin Charles James Fox, and he incurred in consequence the displeasure of Richmond who, though a nominal Whig, was politically narrow-minded and vindictive. Richmond did not like all this flirtation with the Opposition, and what was more he was extremely annoyed by the stories he heard of the part played by his young nephew in the Irish Parliament. There Lord Edward was consistently on the side of Grattan, and although Grattan was by no means a revolutionary, he carried on a steady opposition to the Government. In Richmond's view that was a sort of political betrayal, doubly so as Lord Edward was false to his class; and for his part, Richmond resolved that he was not going to exert himself to advance the military ambitions of his nephew in His Majesty's service.

Still, political worries rest lightly on young shoulders, and the chief preoccupation of Lord Edward in these years was his first love affair. The lady in the case was

Lady Catherine Meade daughter of a recently ennobled
Co. Down landlord who took the title of Earl of Clanwilliam. The course of true love did not run smoothly.
Fitzgerald's nature was constant and affectionate ; what
the young lady's feelings were we do not know, though
any girl must have been flattered by this excess of love
from a man who was in some respects one of the most
eligible bachelors in Dublin. It turned out that there was
one insurmountable obstacle—the mother. Lady Clanwilliam, in the true style of an eighteenth-century mamma,
was on the look out for a young man of guaranteed substance as a husband for her daughter. Younger sons, be
they of ever so exalted a house,she regarded with suspicion.
It was an age when the wealthy needed to be really wealthy.
There were vast rambling country-houses to be maintained,
and there were equally vast town-houses. This required
retinues of servants, and although servants were cheap
one needed a great number. Young Fitzgerald, under
the family settlement, had eight hundred a year ; beyond
this he had only his unknown prospects in the army.
Clanwilliam had intrigued hard to attain his present
position, and it was proper that Lady Catherine should
be maintained in the accustomed style, and not be thrown
away on a young subaltern whose ambition was to go off
campaigning in savage countries. She was pretty, well-
endowed and young and there were several eligible
men about. There was for instance Lord Powerscourt,
owner of great estates in Co. Wicklow and elsewhere.
    There is some evidence that Catherine returned
Fitzgerald's passion, but there was no getting over the
' Dragon '—the nickname Lord Edward applied to her
mother. He confessed his love at great length to his
own mother, and she, kind mamma, was indulgent but
not encouraging, while step-father Ogilvie was frankly
impatient and suggested as a cure that the lad should be
sent to a military academy in London. So, early in 1786,

Lord Edward set out for England, where he entered Woolwich as a military student. He was, or believed he was, deeply enamoured, and he gives a woeful picture of love at the age of twenty-two. He said he got up in the morning hating everything, then he went out intending to call on somebody and forgot whom, with the result that he drifted anywhere at all. He either forgot his dinner engagements or arrived late. He went to bed hating the world and everything, only to arise in the morning to face the hopeless prospect again.

All the time Catherine remained at home in Ireland with the formidable Dragon on guard. Lord Edward's letters home at this period are characteristic of his good-nature. Writing in June 1786 to his mother he says referring to a party. " Lady Clan. will certainly have been there. Are you upon your high horse with her, or are you gracious ? I need not say I hope you are kind to dear pretty Kate, I am sure you are. I want you to like her almost as much as I do ; it is a feeling I always have with people I love excessively. Did you not feel to love her very much and wish for me when you saw her look pretty at the cottage ? " and again a little later, " You cannot conceive how odd the life I lead appears to me. I must confess if I had *le coeur content*, I should like best the idle indolent one. Getting up between 11 and 12, breakfasting in one's jacket *sans souci, se fichant du monde*, and totally careless or thoughtless of everything but the people one loves, is very pleasant *il faut le dire*. I would give a great deal for a lounge at Frescati this morning."

III

Lord Edward spent the summer of 1786 in a trip to the Channel Islands where he accompanied Richmond on an official tour, and in August he returned to Richmond's place at Goodwood. Here he was restless and

wanted badly to go to Ireland, but he professed to be
especially keen on his military studies, and did not like
to return without an excuse. The Channel Islands tour
had in no way turned his mind from Kate. So he wrote
many letters to his mother holding out the suggestion of
an invitation from her to return even for a visit. Influenced by Ogilvie, the Duchess was unmoved and
Edward had to console himself as best he could with the
insipid life at Goodwood and the bleak comforts of
another term at Woolwich, with the distant prospect of
a return to Ireland in January 1787 for the opening of
Parliament. Presently the normal cure for first unrequited
love presented itself, namely second love.

As well as Goodwood, he used occasionally stay at
Stoke, the seat of another uncle, Lord George Lennox.
Here lived his three beautiful cousins, of whom the
youngest was Georgiana. She was aged twenty-one,
and she was gifted not only with beauty, but with that
combination of good-nature and intelligence which goes
very dangerously with beauty. Fitzgerald did not seem
to realise that he was falling in love and believed that
his love for Kate was constant, and that Georgiana did
not really matter. Constancy, he believed, would serve
as defence against all temptation, but for an emotional
young man, whose love had been scorned (at least by
the Dragon) this was a dangerous reliance. The inevitable happened, he soon gave up the struggle of constancy
and when he did succumb, as usual with him, he
succumbed body and soul. Kate leaves the scene and
never reappears, even as a memory, in his life.

There seemed always to be the same prejudice against
younger sons. Old Lennox was if anything more irrascible
than the Dragon, and ended by forbidding his own
nephew the house. This time Fitzgerald seems to have
taken the affair seriously and there is no doubt that he
was genuinely in love. It may be that he reflected bitterly

on the conventions and laws which bind up true love with something so irrelevant as the ownership of property, and a system which hands over a woman at a certain price to the male. The year passed by, there was at least the joy of meeting his mother once again as she was on her way to the Riviera, and Lord Edward spent the winter there with the family. His thoughts meantime were wholly with Georgiana and it was a more reflective youth who returned to Dublin for the opening of Parliament.

five

I

PATRIOTISM, like charity, is a virtue which flourishes best where there are great evils to be remedied. In a complacent land with a benign government it is difficult to be a patriot. But eighteenth-century Ireland was not complacent, and with the failure of Henry Flood's motion for reform, as backed by the Volunteers, the last hopes of a Protestant democracy had disappeared. The political arena to which Edward Fitzgerald returned was noteworthy therefore for the first determined murmurings of extra-parliamentary activity. Here was something entirely new. From the point of view of the administration these movements should have seemed extremely dangerous, for they were organised and directed by the Protestant Anglo-Irish, able and sincere men who were reluctantly driven to this course. Indeed the native Catholic Irish were strangely quiescent, at least so far as activity on a national scale may be reckoned. They confined themselves to fierce agrarian warfare directed against insecure tenures and rack-rents, and above all, against the hated tithes. All the while the Catholic leaders in far-away Dublin trifled with " loyal addresses " and mild proposals for Parliamentary reform, prefacing every diffident plea by an obsequious and almost passionate loyalty to the sacred person of His

Majesty. The provocation of the peasantry was growing intolerable. As Stephen Gwynn remarked " It seems to us nowadays that the devil himself could hardly devise a better means to promote crimes than such a levy " (tithes) ; " and to crown all, Parliament, guided by the landlord interest, made grazing land free of the burden."

There is definate evidence that about this time Lord Edward's opinions were hardening. His gay nature became clouded; what he saw of his fellow-men, combined perhaps with bitterness over his unsuccessful love-suits, gave him a disgust for Irish politics. He ranged himself consistently on the side of Grattan and the small band of the Opposition in Parliament, rather to the annoyance of his brother Leinster, who wavered from Government to Opposition and back again, and to the much greater annoyance of his uncle Richmond. Lord Edward was by no means a rebel or an extremist. Even on tithes—a subject on which he spoke—he would go no further than to urge that some equitable system of collection be devised. But he began to feel that his political position was uncomfortable. His instincts and feelings were all for humanity and justice, but his family, connections and friends would naturally be supporters of the *status quo.*

In those great country houses, at those boring dinner-parties which he was obliged to attend, the universal subject of condemnation was a new theory of government which was said to be gaining currency on the continent. The name of this system was Democracy, and it was supposed to emanate from the devil. It is not surprising that in such surroundings and with such conversation Lord Edward must have felt lonely, have felt indeed that those people were speaking a different language. He complained in a letter that he was greatly disappointed about politics, but not dispirited, and then makes the revealing observation " when one has any great object to carry, one must expect disappointments, and not be diverted from one's object by them, or even appear to mind them ". Could it be that even at this early stage he had formed the idea that "a great object" was sometime to be achieved ? There is at this stage no evidence that he had made any contacts with those extreme elements which were already hinting at armed revolution. He was glad to get away from Ireland, to see his mother once more—she was now resident in England—and to spend the summer of 1787 in a leisurely tour of Spain and Portugal.

II

Parliament met again in the Autumn of 1787 and there were definate signs of the march of events—the beginnings of the *guerre à outrance*. Governments are sometimes glad of a little disorder for it gives them a chance to obtain new powers. Fitzgibbon, the Attorney-General, introduced a Riot Bill designed primarily to deal with the Whiteboy agrarian disturbances in Munster. Once again Fitzgibbon showed himself an impatient realist. He was endeavouring to defend the tithe system and declared that the clergy were not extortioners, that it was impossible for human wretchedness to be greater than it was in Munster, and that the unhappy tenantry were ground to powder by relentless landlords. " I know that, far from being able to give the clergy their dues, they have not raiment for themselves, the landlord grasps the whole ; and sorry I am to add that, not satisfied with the present extortions, some landlords have been base enough to instigate the insurgents to rob the clergy of their tithes, not in order to alleviate the distress of the tenantry, but that they might add the clergy's share to the rackrents already paid." This passage has often been quoted as an indictment of the landlords coming from their staunch friend. But the peculiar cast of Fitzgibbon's mind—and indeed the guiding philosophy of the whole Castle regime—is demonstrated by his attitude to those charges. He declared unequivocally that there must be no remedying unless there is first of all surrender, in other words one must never treat except with people who are abject through terror. This unfortunately became the governing principle of Castle policy and Fitzgibbon would have scorned the thesis that government administration was founded on any principle of fair-play. In his favour it must be conceded that between nation and nation little justice is to be expected unless it is sanctioned by fear, if only the fear of being found out.

Lord Edward was abroad when this session opened and his mind was fixed on one object above all others and this had nothing to do with politics. It was on his return to England in the Autumn of that year that Lord George Lennox, Georgiana's father, forbade him the house. He spent an unhappy and restless winter between Dublin and London and fortunately for him he was able to avail himself of that change which at one time or another suggests itself to most men as the supreme cure for misfortune. He decided to go away to the wilds and leave civilisation behind. He would get away from the villainies of the Irish Parliament, from all the unhappy complications of life in London ; he would ascertain whether the loved image of Georgiana would persist on the other side of the world; he would part even from his beloved mother. It was the remedy of a man who was desperate, but who had nevertheless formed certain standards of value. He could try if solitude, hard living, active employment at all times and escape from what he now perceived were the false securities of civilised living would be of avail. He made what amounted to a secret flight for he did not even acquaint his mother. In May 1788 he took ship to join his regiment, the 54th, then stationed in New Brunswick,

Nova Scotia, in country which was an unreclaimed wilderness. So for the second time the ship sailed westward, bearing a young man who now at twenty-three was more experienced and consequently more embittered.

III

The second sojourn of Fitzgerald in America is recorded for us in a series of letters written to his mother and other members of the family. The theme to which the writer recurs in this correspondence is an impatience with conventions and a hankering for sympathy, for in the early twenties nothing will turn the thoughts to fundamentals like an unsuccessful love-affair. And when failure arises not from rejection by the loved one but because the suitor is a younger son, albeit the son of a premier Duke, it undoubtedly gave scope for speculation on civilised customs.

The voyage took twenty-eight days and he arrived in Halifax in June, 1788 and thence made a long and fatiguing journey to St. John where the regiment was stationed. This journey he described as more like a campaign than anything else, but he now had hopes of a seperate command. In visiting strange places he noted particularly that pattern of life which was close to his own thoughts. The farmer-settlers were as uncouth almost as the Indians, but they were self-supporting and he records that they lived almost entirely within themselves, and this he concluded should make them the happiest people in the world. " The equality of everybody and of their manner of life, I like very much. There are no gentlemen, everybody is on a footing provided he works and wants nothing, every man is exactly what he can make himself." He goes on to give an idyllic picture of an old couple living in a lonely farmstead on the banks of a great river where they had been settled for thirty years. In this remote wilderness there was no living being within sixty miles, and it was hardly an ideal dwelling place in the snows of a Canadian winter. Lord Edward stayed with this old pair for a few nights. There was a busy day on his arrival, but the " contrast of all this which had passed during the day with the quietness of the evening when the spirits of the old people had a little subsided and begun to wear off with the day, and with the fatigue of their little work— sitting quietly at their door, on the same spot they had lived in thirty years together, the contented thoughtful- ness of their countenances which was increased by their age and the solitary life they had led, the wild quietness of the place, not a living creature to be seen and me and Tony and our guide sitting with them on one log. . . The difference of the life I should lead from that of the old pair, perhaps at their age discontented, disappointed and miserable, wishing for power, etc. My dearest mother, if it were not for you I believe I never should go home, at least I thought so at that moment."

He entered with gusto into the busy routine duties of a military officer and he got a small command, one hun- dred miles up river. He got up at five, exercised the men from six to eight, came in to breakfast, from then until three he read, or wrote, and as he says himself settled all the difficult business of the regiment, and dined at four. They paraded again until sundown. Altogether a busy life, but it is noticeable that on more than one occasion he refers to the fact that he reads. What, one wonders, was this busy young officer reading while stationed in the Canadian wilderness ?

Fitzgerald is universally credited with a simplicity and charm of character, readily admitted even by political enemies, but it is not usual to credit him with any intel- lectual endowments. This judgement is undeserved. When quite young he acquired a taste for reading and he

was an early admirer of Rousseau. His mother despite
eye-trouble was also a great reader. Afterwards, when he
had returned to London, she records that amid the distractions of the capital Edward was leading a quiet life
reading Milton, and as we shall see, he was a close student
of Tom Paine. He arrived at convictions foreign to his
upbringing and self-interest, and he felt these things so
deeply, that in the end he hazarded all even life itself in
defence of them.

Probably Rousseau was the favourite at this stage
though the *Social Contract* is not perhaps the ideal bedside
book for a young man stationed a hundred miles up-river in
Canada. There are several passages in his letters which
show that if he did read Rousseau he read him with interest
and profit. Like many others he was much taken by the
chances of instinctive happiness in a life of primitive simplicity but he did not pass to the more profound reflection
that for modern man, particularly if he is educated, such
simplicity must be sophisticated. No man can ignore the
requirements of the mind when once they are awakened,
hence perhaps the essential flaw in taking Rousseau too
literally.

Many people who freely recognise the shams of conventional living are perforce prepared to accept them,
but Lord Edward was in his first enthusiasm. " I know "
he writes, " Ogilvie says I ought to have been a savage
and if it were not that the people I love and wish to live
with are civilised people and like houses, etc. I really
would join the savages ; and leaving all our fictitious,
ridiculous wants, be what nature intended we should be.
Savages have all the real happiness of life without any of
those inconveniences or ridiculous obstacles to it which
custom has introduced amongst us. They enjoy the love
and company of their wives, relations and friends without
any interference of interests or ambition to separate them
. . . Instead of Lord George Lennox being violent against

letting me marry Georgiana, he would be glad to give her to me that I might maintain and feed her. There would be then no cases of looking forward to the fortune of children—of thinking how you are to live ; no separation of families, one in Ireland, one in England ; no devilish politics, no fashions, customs, duties, or appearances to the world, to interfere with one's happiness. Instead of being served and supported by servants everything here is done by one's relations and the mutual obligations you must be under increase your love for each other. To be sure the poor ladies are obliged to cut a little wood and to bring in a little water. Now the dear Ciss and Mimi, instead of being with Mrs. Lynch, would be carrying wood and fetching water, while ladies Lucy and Sophia were cooking or drying fish. As for you dear mother, you would be smoking your pipe."

It is evident too that Lord Edward was impressed by what he fancied were principles of equality. These were the years immediately preceding the French Revolution when the war cry was adopted of Liberty, Equality and Fraternity—in that order. The terms served as a slogan, but one who, like Lord Edward, reflected on these things may have felt that liberty and equality are not ideals easy of achievement in the human order. It is possible that there is no such thing as absolute liberty. Economic equality is achieved by the comparatively easy process of an equal diffusion of wealth, but when this is accomplished, and it is not accomplished even yet, it will then be time enough to face the inequalities arising from taste, intellectual endowment, and temperament. This is the supreme problem which faces civilisation when the comparatively simple state of economic egalitarianism is accomplished.

There was however much that was accurate in Lord Edward's reflections. For instance the unequal diffusion of wealth has been probably the greatest single cause of human misery—greater than tyrannical governments, for those latter have always existed to maintain it. It was the root-cause of the Irish horror which Fitzgerald and his brethren afterwards set out to destroy, though they and their successors for a hundred years were more concerned with the formalities of constitutional government. Fitzgerald wrote feelingly of that equality which would render titles of honour (like his own) absurd. He did not venture to speculate whether even then there might not be the need of some form of aristocracy to take the place of these debauched landowners who were fated to be overthrown; an aristocracy, to use Mr. E. M. Forster's phrase "consisting of the sensitive, the considerate and the plucky."

IV

The Canadian winter fell with its usual severity and the country became snowbound. Lord Edward, young vigourous and happy, despite his yearning for Georgiana, made ready to enjoy the winter. He procured his snowshoes and all the necessary gear for hunting, and his mind was diverted by letters from home. " I really do think " he wrote " there is no luxury equal to that of lying before a good fire, on a good spruce bed, after a good supper and a hard moose chase in a fine clear frosty moonlight starry night ". Or again " If Georgiana should love me when I go home I shall be the happiest fellow in the world."

It seems incongruous that the petty worries from outside should penetrate into this snowbound backwood, but such it was. There were two matters in particular to trouble the absent member of Parliament. Firstly Leinster had gone over from the popular side to the Government, and Lord Edward, being his nominated member, would be expected to go over with him. Secondly Richmond had suddenly become effusively friendly and was talking about a lieutenant-colonelcy. The circumstances of Leinster's defection had better be left until we return to deal with affairs in Ireland. As for Richmond, Lord Edward was really perturbed; he began to feel that somehow there was a plot. As he saw it, he was to be a supporter of the Government and all else would follow. The persuasion would be gentle. He need not do anything discreditable, he need not give any pledges, nor render himself prominent or aggressive, and being a nominated member he could say he was bound, according to the conventions of the day, to vote as his patron bade him. Yet even in the Canadian solitudes he was horrified by the idea and it is evident that his opinions had taken definite shape. He wrote hastily to his stepfather, Ogilvie, and he wrote to his mother asking her to beg Ogilvie to do nothing about the lieutenant-colonelcy as he was determined to have no promotion or rewards till he was out of Parliament. " I have no ambition for rank and however I might be flattered by getting on, it would never pay me for a blush for my actions. The feeling of shame is what I could never bear. The *mens conscia recti* is the only thing that makes life supportable."

He then received a long letter from his uncle Richmond. The Duke proceeded to argue in affable terms that as Leinster had gone over completely to the Government, he could not after all see any reason why Edward could not act with his brother. Lord Edward was Leinster's nominee and Richmond hinted at something which for one with the strong family feeling of Lord Edward had a peculiar terror—a " family schism." Lord Edward could not see a way out of the difficulty at the moment as he was still a Member, so he replied to Richmond and said that in the circumstances he would act with Leinster. But to his mother he wrote that he believed Leinster in the wrong and had told him so beforehand, and reiterated significantly that now when he had agreed to support Leinster he

was determined not to take anything, lieutenant-colonelcy
or anything else.   After this rather unhappy exchange he
set out on an adventurous journey to Quebec and spent
most of the winter shooting moose.

In April, 1789 Lord Edward wrote to Ogilvie that he
expected to get away in June, but he had decided on a
tour down the Mississippi to New Orleans. He set out
in May, going first to see Niagara which impressed him in
a somewhat unusual way by the contrasting tranquility
of everything about ; the quiet of the immense forests
around compared with the violence of all that is close
to the Falls. He was adopted into an Indian tribe. He
kept going, partly by canoe, partly by any other means
available, journeying on through the scorching heat of
a mid-American summer, through country that was only-
half-explored, and reached New Orleans in November.
He contemplated a trip to South America, but there was
one attraction, powerful almost as life itself, which turned
his thoughts towards home. Also there was the risk of a
Spanish war. He decided therefore to go home, soon he
could embrace his mother, and perhaps, who could tell,
lapse of time might have changed the ideas of Lord
George Lennox about suitable provision, and Georgiana,
to whom in all the vicissitudes of the American wilderness
his thoughts turned night and day, might yet be his
bride.   He would soon be with her, and that at least
would be true happiness.

At this point he received a shock which may have con-
firmed his views on civilised living, a shock so profound
and so terrible that it may truthfully be said to have
changed his whole outlook on life and to have altered the
pattern of his career. As far back as the previous April
the beautiful Georgiana had been quietly married to Lord
Bathurst ; while Lord Edward in New Orleans was
waiting in joyful anticipation of seeing her soon, she was
in fact already four months married.

SIX

I

MEANTIME in Ireland there had been a session of Parliament remarkable for the three-months affair known as the Regency Crisis.

In the autumn of 1788 strange stories about the King's health came from across the Channel. The King went to Cheltenham to recuperate, and in November the doctors issued the ominous bulletin—the King was insane. This caused great excitement in the Whig camp and equally there was dismay amongst Pitt's followers. The reason was simple. George, Prince of Wales, would be Regent; ' Prinny ' the intimate friend of Fox and Sheridan the habitué of Devonshire House, and the enemy of the Tories. What more natural than that in due course, in exercise of unquestioned constitutional right, he would sweep the Tories from office and in their place install his friends. Thus unexpectedly the Whigs would be in power and the idea was intoxicating. Already the leaders were sharing out the great offices between themselves. Amongst other things, for example, it was arranged that Richard Brinsley Sheridan, who for nearly twenty years had been mismanaging his own finances and endeavouring not very successfully to keep the bailiffs at bay, was to become Chancellor of the Exchequer, a proposal which with equal lack of humour was afterwards changed to Treasurer of the Navy.

In Ireland the news, if possible, caused even greater perturbation. The British Whigs, it must be said, had always been friendly to the liberal hopes of Grattan, Flood and the Opposition party generally. In this they were sincere, and indeed there is evidence that the Whigs believed that the Grattanites should travel more quickly towards democracy and particularly towards the enfranchisement of the Catholics. The Government faction trembled, they saw not only that the end was near but that they were ruined for all time. What, it may be asked, had become of their supporters in Parliament whom they had bought and paid for so well ? These worthy gentlemen almost to a man made it clear that they could not support the Government on any matter touching the limitation of Regency powers. They were quite logical, if one is to change allegiance it is of the greatest importance to change in good time.

But the end was not quite yet. In Britain the Tories had found after some manoeuvering that they might be obliged to give up without even making a fight for it. But their dejected friends in Ireland gathered new hope, though a slender one. Two facts were clear which seemed at first sight to be fatal to any resistance by the Castle. The claim, or to be more accurate the right, of the Prince to act as Regent could not be by-passed, and secondly the Regent had a legal right to exercise the royal prerogative of calling for a change of government. Nevertheless the constitutional lawyers got busy and difficulties and delays arose. There were scarcely any precedents save some of doubtful analogy in the time of the Plantagenets when certain kings were minors or had fled the realm. A king overtly mad had never yet sat on the English throne. There was also the curious difficulty that Parliament at the moment could not legislate since Parliament comprised the three Estates of which the sovereign was one ; the existing sovereign was still on the throne, but incapacitated by illness from exercising assent, and until this Estate could be supplied by some other means Parliament could not proceed by way of legislation. The most it could do was to present an Address, and an Address therefore was the Whig strategem, for laws could not be enacted by way of an Address.

In Britain Pitt and his followers were anxious—if it it could be done—to limit in some way the new Regent's powers. This would require legislation and accordingly they procured Thurlow, the Lord Chancellor, to devise a fantastic and illegal procedure for attaching the Royal Assent. The Parliamentary debates—full of metaphysics and the abstractions and fictions of the constitution— were long and wearisome ; each side knew exactly what the other was after, but both professed to be concerned only with the niceties of legality.

In Ireland the question was even more complicated, the additional factors being the common sovereign and the exercise of certain of his powers by the Lord Lieutenant. It was emphasised both by the Government and by the Opposition that Ireland was an independent Kingdom, and that the sole link connecting her with England was the unity of the Crown. Any straining at that unity, such for example as divergent powers for a Regent in Ireland, or, as was possible, a different Regent, might lead to total separation. Fitzgibbon warned the country gentlemen who made up the Commons to take good care of what it was they were about. He detailed as a last resort an argument which struck home and struck deeply, In a remarkable speech he reminded the members that anything might happen if the protection of the English connection were lost. The gentlemen were plainly disturbed, they were hesitant but somehow they decided to risk it. Fitzgibbon's threats were remote but there was no doubt as to the immediate advent of a new Government, and politically it is wise to be on the winning side. But the Castle junta had grown desperate, and unlike the English Government, they decided to fight to the last. There were some strange developments.

The Irish Parliament passed an Address humbly praying the Prince to take on himself the regency of the realm. But the junta procured that their friend Buckingham, the Lord Lieutenant, would refuse to transmit the Address to the Prince on the grounds that the Prince was still a subject, George III being as yet the sovereign. Parliament, incensed, took the drastic step of passing a vote of censure on Buckingham and appointing their own delegates to wait on the Prince. The delegates (one of whom was the Duke of Leinster) were received graciously in London and returned triumphantly to await events. Then there was anti-climax—uneasy rumours that the King was recovering, one eminent doctor declaring that he was cured while another declared that his malady was incurable. The first was denounced by the Whigs as being in the pay of the Tories, as for the other the Tories said that he was a quack.

The King did in fact recover, and the sighs of relief that went up from the Castle in Dublin must have been audible all over the city. It remained only to wreak vengeance and to distribute rewards, and to this congenial task Fitzgibbon and his followers set themselves with a will. It was seen that the defection of placemen had been on such a scale that wholesale massacre was impracticable ; there was therefore a compromise. The ringleaders were excepted but an amnesty was declared for those pensioners and office-holders who would return to the fold. Amongst those dismissed was Leinster who lost his sinecure of Master of the Rolls, and who once again joined the popular ranks. Amongst the rewards for loyal service was the preferment of Fitzgibbon, who, after much importunity both in England and Ireland, was appointed Lord Chancellor with

the title of Lord Clare—the first born Irishman to hold
the post for over a century. At forty he had reached
what seemed to be the apex of a career but he was yet to
play a prominent, and discreditable, part in the tragic
history of his country.

II

All seemed set for a steady régime of spoliation and
repression ; but the year was 1789, and once again
strange and disquieting news came from across the sea ;
this time however from France. The Bastille had fallen
and the long convulsion of the French Revolution had
begun. The French masses called on the oppressed
people of every land to join them. This call in due
course reached Ireland and was taken up, not—as one
might expect—by the degraded masses of the Catholic
peasants, but here and there by groups of men, Protestants
mostly, some of them aristocrats and landowners and some
of them mild intellectuals. This was a new sort of threat
with which the English connection had never yet had to
reckon, a revolutionary movement amongst the educated
Anglo-Irish middle-class.

Fitzgibbon now had a new recruit whom he brought
over from the Opposition, Robert Stewart, Viscount
Castlereagh, a young man (the same age as Edward
Fitzgerald) of handsome person and with a talent for
intrigue and affairs, and who was later to win fame in a
wider sphere. He was the son of a recently ennobled
northern landowner who, like, himself, had deserted the
popular side and received a title. Fitzgibbon taught
Castlereagh the political value of lack of scruple and
this he was destined to exploit to the full in Irish affairs.
These two now addressed themselves, after the amazing
deliverance from the Regency crisis, to consolidating the
Ascendancy. It was easy work. But they took scant

F

note of a new movement, begun in a small way, which swelled to a nation-wide effort and which united Protestant Anglo-Irish, Presbyterian, and Catholic. For a long time the entire constitutional structure of the Kingdom was threatened, until the vision of a democratic republic faded out in betrayal and disaster. The year 1791 saw the foundation of the Society of United Irishmen.

III

Lord Edward arrived in London early in 1790 his mother and most of his family being then resident there. He was now aged twenty-five and it was at this point in life that fate intervened with an improbability which might be deemed inadmissible in fiction. Three things—not seemingly connected—combined to decide his future. The first was the marriage of his beloved Georgiana Lennox. No one ever dies of a broken heart or of unrequited love and if one is to judge by Lord Edward's correspondence at this time the effect on him, so far as was compatible with his generous nature, was to render him hard and cynical—at least for a time. He bravely affected to laugh and make light of the matter, but there is no doubt that the shock his nature received predisposed him to extreme courses away from the pattern of life of those people nearest his heart ; and he felt a digust for many things which friends and relatives considered valuable.

The second event was a general election in Ireland in 1788 ; a rather significant election, for a new Whig Club had been formed in Dublin and Grattan and Lord Edward's own brother, Lord Henry Fitzgerald, had won Dublin for the popular cause, an event marked by illuminations all over the city. Without his knowledge and, it is said, against the wishes of his mother the Duke of Leinster once more returned Lord Edward as Member for Athy, although at this time he had made it clear that he had no wish for Parliamentary entanglements. However the deed was done, but he seems to have been unaware of this when he landed in England.

The third event had immediate consequences and deserves treatment in some detail. Very soon after his arrival in England Fitzgerald went to see his uncle Richmond, and the Duke, beaming all over announced that he had great news. The war with Spain which had been so much talked about while Fitzgerald was in America was now a reality. Since 1789 England was at war. As in so many previous wars with the same Power it was decided to make a descent on Cadiz, and Richmond had the astounding news that it was proposed to give the command of this expedition—or rather raiding-party—to Lord Edward. The nephew fairly reeled with excitement. Here at last, and most unexpectedly, was a chance of that military adventure of which for years he had dreamt. He was just in the mood for it too. He was recovering from a broken love-affair, he wished to get away from England and all the places where he might chance to run into Georgiana, her husband or her friends ; and in no circumstances did he wish to return to Ireland and become involved in Parliamentary intrigues or associate with a gang of placemen or pensioners. Here then was the cure for every evil—an exciting and dangerous expedition to Cadiz and a chance of glory.

The history of this transaction is illuminating. One afternoon Richmond took Fitzgerald to see no less a pair than William Pitt the Prime Minister, and Dundas the Home Secretary. Pitt explained that the authorities were impressed by the account received of Fitzgerald's military career so far, and then and there offered him the brevet of the command against Cadiz. The matter, he explained, was to go next day to the King himself to have the commission signed. There were some polite suggestions, seemingly afterthoughts, that a person holding such an important command, would be expected not to be found in opposition to His Majesty's Government in Ireland. To these hints Fitzgerald paid no attention. He believed himself not to be in Parliament at the time and he had no intention of ever standing again. It did not concern him therefore what these Ministers believed to be the proper standard of conduct for a Member of Parliament. The important thing was the military expedition ; once embarked upon that politics and everything connected with them would be far from his mind. He went home in those high spirits which come so rarely in life ; feeling that elation which comes to one who knows that after many disappointments and strivings his chance has come at last.

The next day things began to happen. He was to call on Richmond, he was to see Dundas again, possibly to see Pitt and even the King himself. But before he set out on this impressive assignment he received one small bit of news which made a material change. The previous summer—1788—as we have seen, his brother Leinster had returned him to Parliament. Fitzgerald suddenly saw the whole affair as a trick. Richmond had long since disapproved of his radical views, and he hoped that Lord Edward's support could be bought by an offer of army promotion. In conversations with his sister, the Dowager Duchess of Leinster, Richmond must have gathered that this was a hopeless venture. Lord Edward would not be bought, and the Duchess may have quoted to him those passages from the letters which show how deep was Lord Edward's resolve. What then was to be done with this erring young radical who held a valuable seat in the Irish Commons?

It is difficult to sort out motives or even to be sure of the sequence of events, yet it is impossible to rule out something like a plot. Why was the important news that

he had again been returned to Parliament kept from
Lord Edward, who was then several weeks in London
and was in daily contact with his relatives and connections?
It can scarcely have been because they did not know about
it, because the Duchess at least had been consulted by her
son Leinster and she had disapproved of his action in returning Lord Edward to Parliament. The latter made up
his mind instantly. He sought out Richmond and in an
angry interview told him that he would not accept the
Cadiz appointment. This instant refusal is important as it
shows a character with deep convictions. He had not as
yet formed any definite views about Irish politics, but
he was determined at least that he would not be a supporter
of the Government at any price.

It is instructive to reflect on the extent of the sacrifice. He had been offered what to him was a dazzling
prize, glorious in itself and the prelude to greater military
achievement. It was precisely that active and daring work
which his present frustrated and restless mood demanded.
It would have healed all wounds and utilised all energies.
In return he had merely to refrain from active opposition
to Government legislation in Ireland. On the face of it
this did not appear a severe demand. Parliament met
only every two years for a short session and possibly,
as when in Canada, he would be abroad; he was not
therefore committed very deeply. Or, as had happened
on one or two occasions, the Government might become
benevolent and proceed to popular legislation.

To refuse this offer and hold himself free for opposition
was to close the door once and for all on that career which
he felt was the only life for him. Few men care to bid a
final adieu to cherished ambitions, for Lord Edward the
blow was especially severe. It meant that at twenty-six
he was to face a pointless and humdrum existence, length-
ening out into untold stretches of boredom and idleness.
He had few other resources. He was not, like his cousin

Fox, a unique combination of gambling-man and scholar. He never acquired a taste for dissipation or high-living, and he disliked the sort of life that went on in the great drawing-rooms of Leinster House or Carton, or in England at Goodwood and Devonshire House. Perhaps, most poignant thought of all, his mother would be displeased.

He had made his choice instantly and all was over. The command was withdrawn. He was free now for a few months until the Irish Parliament sat in the summer. He spent the time in London and determined if possible to be cheerful, and gay months they were on the whole. But it was with gloomy thoughts that the young man crossed the Channel to attend Parliament. He detested the corrupt atmosphere of Irish parliamentary life; yet, somewhat to his surprise, he was gradually to discover new interest there. When he reflected on conditions in Ireland he was horrified. Here he discovered was a chance to apply those abstract notions of equality and justice of which he wrote so much from Canada.

In France liberty and equality had now been proclaimed and never was a country more in need of them than Ireland. Lord Edward began to think that his great friend Henry Grattan did not go nearly far enough. He heard that there were other men in Dublin, men outside Parliament, outside the normal walk of political life, who dealt in remedies which Parliament could not give. In Parliament there was always a number of limitations ; even Grattan, honourable and upright as he was, believed profoundly in monarchy, landlords, property qualifications and the British connection. All remedies must, according to him, be framed within these limits. But there were dark stories of influential men in Dublin to whom such things meant nothing. They were prepared to strike at the very roots ;   the first thing that must go was the British connection, upon which the whole edifice of corruption and oppression depended.

seven

I

POLITICAL affairs in Ireland were now, so to speak, running in separate streams. Firstly there was Parliament itself, which met for a short session in July 1790. On a previous occasion, not so many years before, the Government had been frightened by the importunities of the Volunteers. That threat had been dealt with, the Volunteers as an organised unit did not now exist. But a new menace, it seemed, was now appearing.

The Catholics numbered three-fourths of the population, and any concrete and intelligently directed effort by them was a thing which was really dangerous; and they were now organised and making insistent demands. That was the second stream. Another stream of activity had not gathered full force, but it was something as yet unheard of in Ireland—it was revolution.

At this time there lived in Dublin a medical doctor named William Drennan. He came originally from the North, being a native of Co. Down, and his people were Presbyterians. He had many friends and connections in the North particularly amongst those with radical views. As a doctor he was reckoned average, but he was a man of wide vision and advanced and enlightened outlook.

During his medical residence in Edinburgh he had associated with men whose views were embodied in the *Rights of Man*, Scotland at this date being noted for revolutionary thought.   Drennan was moreover an able pamphleteer ; and he has left a series of letters dealing chiefly with the political trends of his day, together with some patriotic verse.   His one foible was a preoccupation with cabalistic ritual which was to prove a source of annoyance to his associates in the revolutionary movement.

Drennan was connected with the Whig Club in Dublin but like others he was dissatisfied with its conservative atmosphere.   In Dublin Grattan was the recognised leader of the popular Opposition and he was by no means leftist in his views.   Outside Parliament the other great leaders were the heads of the Catholic movement.   They however were strongly opposed to any revolutionary ideas and were constantly professing their humble devotion to His Majesty and the Constitution, and meanwhile their bishops declared that anyone who sympathised with the ideas of the French Revolution was guilty of grave sin.

Dublin obviously was no place for subversive doctrines but in Belfast the case was different.   In the Northern town radical opinions were flourishing.   There the fall of the Bastille was annually celebrated with ceremony and there also men gathered together in little organised groups to discuss ways and means of implementing the Rights of Man in their own country.   They were, comparatively speaking, moderate in their demands, they were not seeking any separation from England but it was soon apparent that they were not content to be moderate and legalist as to means.   If all else failed and if the Junta was so firmly entrenched that they could not otherwise be moved, then force would be used.   However threats of force were as yet a long way off.   But an interesting point is that the groups were concerned almost exclusively with what we should now call political justice, that is to say equitable representation and responsible government. There was as yet no suggestion of a redistribution of property.

Drennan, exiled in the conservative atmosphere of Dublin, was much interested in these developments. He kept up a constant correspondence, particularly with his brother-in-law McTier in Belfast. In May, 1791 he sent McTier an interesting memorandum in which he outlined a scheme for the formation of a new and radical 'brotherhood' which was to work by political methods for the Rights of Man, for the " greatest happiness of the greatest number," for the independence of Ireland and a republican form of government. This document was also circulated amongst left-wing friends in Dublin. There Drennan's views were taken up eagerly by an able and energetic young barrister named Theobald Wolfe Tone, at this time secretary to the Catholic Committee. Tone also looked to Belfast as the home of republican opinion and, like Drennan, he had a correspondent there, a great friend named Thomas Russell. This Russell was a handsome young man with a singular nobility of character in whose radicalism there was combined more than a touch of mysticism. He had been an army officer and a magistrate but abandoned both professions in deference to his principles.

Hearing of the interest in Belfast in Drennan's memorandum, Tone wrote to Russell enclosing an outline scheme for the Movement and adding a postscript which identified the Movement as separatist and republican. Tone was thereupon commissioned to draft the scheme of the new Society (as the organisation was to be called) and went to Belfast with this draft. There, at a meeting, the memorandum was discussed with some of McTier's friends. These discussions and some further correspondence took place and there came into being that organisation which was to renew the forlorn struggle for

Irish independence; the Society the very name of which even to-day moves Irishmen deeply, the Society of United Irishmen.

II

The Society of United Irishmen was the most serious movement as yet with which the Castle had to reckon because the central and essential feature was a union of Catholic and Protestant, of Anglo-Irish and ' old ' Irish. Soon the Belfast enthusiasm spread to Dublin, Wolfe Tone and his friend Russell formed the Dublin Society of United Irishmen and new leaders appeared. The Society had fairly good backing at first, men of substance like Simon Butler, Napper Tandy and Hamilton Rowan came over from the Whig Club and in July 1791 there was a parade in Stephen's Green to celebrate the fall of the Bastille. The immediate possibility was that the United Irishmen might link up with the already existing Catholic movement, for by 1792 the Catholic agitation under the leadership of a wealthy poplin merchant named John Keogh had gathered great force and Wolfe Tone was acting as secretary. Nevertheless the purpose of this Catholic movement was not so much to bring about Parliamentary reform—not to speak or Revolution—as to abolish what remained of the penal laws.

This penal code which figures so prominently in the history of the period calls for some mention, even at the risk of digression. There is nothing unusual in religious intolerance, yet, of its kind, the Irish penal code was unique. The British, to give them their due, have always been half-hearted when it came to religious persecution. This was a typical British compromise, because religion is essentially such a personal matter, that in a last analysis it cannot be persecuted at all. As a nation, the British have been unable to work up an interest in religious controversy; exhortation leaves them reverent but unmoved. Hence, not since the time of Queen Mary has anyone been condemned for the profession of a particular religion as such. Even the redoubtable Cromwell said " I interfere with no man's conscience ". But this same people developed a liking for an awkward doctrine known as uniformity. Thus a man could profess any religion he liked—or none—without breaking the law, but Parliament none the less could provide certain " tests ", and if these were not complied with a citizen could, for example, be excluded from holding offices or privileges. It is obvious that if used without restraint this exclusion could be an outrageous form of persecution. The conscience of the time saw nothing wrong in this, perhaps because much of the law was in abeyance, and " abeyance ", within the British legislative system, is, if possible, a more effective oblivion than actual repeal. The feeling for uniformity survived until the late nineteenth-century when Charles Bradlaugh was excluded from Parliament for refusing to make what for him was an obnoxious and superstitious declaration.

It may be argued that the majority felt entitled to protect itself against subversive activities and religious doctrines. Dissenters, for instance, tended to be republican and socialist, while Catholics were nearly always Jacobites. It will be found, however, upon examination, that religious persecution is founded on economic interest. It has something to do with property rights, or with jobs. It never derives from an excess of zeal for the gentle teachings of the Master. This has been the case as far back as the persecution of the early Christians by Nero and the other Emperors. Those Christians were a new and terrifying menace; they were communist sectaries who proclaimed an equality and brotherhood of all men under God. They held that wealth was an evil thing; that it was well-nigh impossible for a rich man to be saved, and they claimed that the pronouncements of the Saviour were unequivocal about this. Rome was a slave-holding and parasitic State; naturally these doctrines with their universal appeal were calculated to put, literally, the fear of God in the hearts of the ruling-class. The terror inspired by the Christian teaching accounts for the utter ferocity of the Roman persecution. There was no question of solicitude for the ancient beliefs.

In time, as we know, Christian teaching was modified, and came to be compatible with the ownership of great wealth, as it is in our own day. When one reads, therefore, that a Ruler is " persecuting religion " it is as well to be cautious, since all experience shows that Governments encourage the practice of religion amongst their subjects. It will be found invariably that there is some question of proprietary rights involved. So, there have been many persecutions since Roman times, and some of the most savage were conducted by Christians against other Christians.

In eighteenth-century Ireland, the attempt to turn people away from Rome had long since been abandoned, but it was seen that the laws served a new and unexpected purpose, namely to maintain the property-rights of the minority. Thus there were severe restrictions on the leasing and ownership of land. The entire patronage of the State was reserved to the minority, for the Catholics could hold no public office or commissions in the army. Deprived of educational facilities, they could never hope to enter any profession, and in any event all professions, except medicine, were closed to them. The laws directed against religious practice, as such, were not enforced, but the property laws were retained and enforced until the end of the eighteenth century. When one hears sentimental remarks about the beauties of the heritage of Georgian Dublin, it is instructive to reflect that this splendour depended not merely on exploitation by a small class—which is a normal feature of human affairs—but on exploitation maintained by a particularly mean and fraudulent pretence. The suffering caused by the penal code was of peculiar intensity. The laws were relentless and at times ruthlessly applied, and the effect over a century was devastating. John Keogh, the Catholic leader, said in 1790 that you could recognise a Catholic from the cringing way in which he walked through the streets, and traces of this servility can be observed in Ireland to the present day.

When the time came, Ireland owed her deliverance from the code to two external causes. The American War brought independence to the Irish Parliament; the French Revolution was the indirect cause of justice and equality for the Catholics. The Pope and Catholic interests generally were powerful forces in the war against the French, and Pitt, their ally, conveyed a meaning hint to the Irish Government that the Catholics should forthwith be placated. Nothing much was done, although in 1788 and 1792 there were partial relief acts in Ireland, and in 1791 a complete Act in England.

The existing Catholic Committee—the representative body of the Catholics—had behaved disgracefully. It was dominated by aristocratic elements and by the more conservative of the hierarchy, and the Committee was uncomfortable that any reliefs should be deemed as flowing from the atheistic principles of the French Revolution. So strong was this feeling that they took the incredible course of informing the Government that the Catholics did not want any further reliefs. There was naturally great indignation amongst the Catholic rank-and-file and amongst many of their Protestant fellow-citizens as well. A revolt took place, the aristo-crats and anathematizing bishops were thrown out, John Keogh became leader, and Theobald Wolfe Tone, a Protestant, was appointed secretary. Tone then

published an ably-written and lucid pamphlet entitled:
An Argument on behalf of the Catholics of Ireland.

The leader knew that their case was unchallengeable
and that three-quarters of the citizens, possibly more,
were supporting them. Confident of this backing they
decided on a bold plan of action. Keogh and Tone
stumped the country organising a ' Catholic Convention '
which was to be held in Dublin and which would have
all the appearance of a representative legislative assembly.
This Convention assembled in the autumn of 1792.
There was at that date nothing illegal in this procedure
and there was nothing that the authorities could do to
interfere, yet the Castle junta felt decidedly nervous.
Here was a representative assembly speaking for three-
fourths of the nation while the legitimate Parliament
sitting nearby was by contrast merely a rump. It was
a tangible demonstration of strength. The Convention
unfortunately had not lost the habit of the ' loyal
address ' but even in this degrading procedure another
hard blow was dealt at the ascendancy. It was decided
to by-pass the Lord Lieutenant and to proceed direct
to the King in person. This was an astute move, for
a favourable reception was assured across the water.
Delegates were selected who travelled to England by
way of Belfast, and it was on this occasion that the
carriages bearing the Catholic leaders were drawn through
the streets of Belfast by the enthusiastic dissenters of the
North.

The whole movement was crowned with complete
success. The petition borne by the delegates admitted no
compromise or half-measures, it asked simply for complete equality for Catholics with the rest of His Majesty's
loyal subjects. Dundas the Home Secretary was sympathetic—perhaps sincerely so—and asked for the petition,
undertaking that he himself would lay it before the King.
Keogh however said " No ! " They had had enough of

that sort of evasiveness in Ireland. They had made the dramatic gesture of coming to London to petition His Majesty in person and speaking for over three-fourths of His Majesty's subjects in Ireland they would not leave until admitted to the royal presence, the King in English Constitutional theory being the fountain of justice. Dundas had to agree and the interview was arranged.

Various accounts are given of the remarkable interview which took place at St. James's Palace on January 2nd, 1793 ; of how the delegates, including Keogh, were so suitably attired for the occasion, and of how graciously they were received by the King who greeted each in turn. The results were swift, complete and decisive. Instructions were conveyed to the Irish Government, and the following session saw legislation to remove the last disabilities on Roman Catholics and admit them to full equality. The holding of certain offices was excepted and of course Catholics could not sit in Parliament unless they took an oath which to them was obnoxious. This disability survived for a further thirty years but by then the Irish Parliament was no more. For practical purposes however the legislation of 1793 saw the end of the penal laws.

III

Yet the national grievances that remained were deep and terrible. Equality for Catholics was a mockery if there was no reform of Parliament, and legislation and the administration of affairs was still in the hands of a small clique. It was here that the radical leaders stepped in, and their path was clearly outlined. Parliament could be reformed only by itself, there was no other legal machinery for the purpose. But the majority in Parliament was stubbornly resolved that there would be no reform and the majority was bought by the Government. Here was an impasse from which there was no escape, and indeed the outbreak of the war with France merely strengthened the hands of the Government for they suppressed the Volunteers as an irregular body and branded as treason any trafficking in theories and methods which originated in France. The Irish progressive movement therefore went underground and the United Irishmen became a secret oathbound Society. There was nothing for it but to prepare for the struggle if democracy and equality were to become a reality. The leaders began to look for help to that country which bade all oppressed peoples to arise. None could have a stronger case than the United Irishmen and, with a brief pause in 1795, events marched steadily to the climax of civil war.

eight

I

THE spacious windows of Devonshire House looked over the Green Park. This great house was the fashionable centre of the Whig world, a distinction shared later on with Holland House further west in Kensington. Devonshire House, however, was strongly influenced by the female element, and Georgiana Duchess of Devonshire, was the representative figure. Her chief associates were a sister, Lady Bessborough, and a dubious friend Lady Elizabeth Foster, the latter amongst other things being the Duke of Devonshire's mistress. Here the leaders of the Party gathered, chief of whom was Charles James Fox, together with a host of Whig camp-followers and rising young men. Here also came Richard Brinsley Sheridan, who was born in Dublin the son of an Irish elocution teacher. He was now aged forty, and for twenty years he had pursued a brilliant and distracted career in London. The Prince of Wales frequently visited from Carlton House. The Prince believed himself an ill-treated man, the victim of many misfortunes, beset by creditors and harried by discarded mistresses. He was therefore a man of several worries. In Devonshire House he found Whig ears ready to listen to his plaint, and people who

agreed in tracing all his sorrows to the misdeeds of his
doddering parents.

The Whigs believed in ' freedom ' and flirted with
French democracy and they read or pretended to have
read Voltaire and Rousseau.   It is to be presumed that
these political theories and this yearning for the primitive
hedonism of the savage affected their private lives.   The
ideas took a practical shape not noticeable for originality.
The Whigs were rich men, the gambling was prodigious,
while the love-making was such that there was a whole
tribe of children of the mist, and subsequent historians
have not quite succeeded in sorting them out.   The
Duchess of Devonshire, the presiding hostess, had a
lover, Sir George Grey (afterwards Earl Grey) to whom
she bore a child, while the Duke had two children by
Lady Elizabeth Foster.   This latter nobleman worked
on a pragmatic principle.   If his own amours were
unmolested he was disposed not to be censorious of his
wife—provided that she did not overdo it.   In such case
he might feel obliged to exert a little marital proprietor-
ship.   So, when the affairs of his spouse became blatant,
she was banished to France; later, however, she returned
to reign with undiminished vigour at Devonshire House.

The dissipations in general were not marked by
refinement, and tastes were not fastidious.   Fox by his
gambling contrived to exhaust two large fortunes, and
then he set up in business himself by opening a faro
bank in Brooks's, where, strangely enough, he made
some money.   In the annals of debts and borrowing it
was an age of titans, and in this department the achieve-
ments of Fox have become proverbial, exceeding those
even of Brinsley Sheridan.   Indeed the crowning exploit
of Charles James Fox was that he actually borrowed
from Sheridan himself.   Most of the men however were
idle and bored, they drank enormously and they over-ate
as well.   They were in consequence nearly all decrepit

at forty, suffering from strange diseases usually put down as ' gout '. One gentleman, Lord Carlisle, averred that his gout was due to the fact that of late his life had been too chaste and he resolved to remedy the omission, arriving by this indirect route at that ancient heresy that chastity is the least commendable of the virtues.

II

This was the society into which Edward Fitzgerald as the cousin of Fox and connection of Whig notables had a ready entry. During the succeeding two years he lived chiefly in London and it is not surprising that a young man with his introduction should have found London more attractive than Dublin. His mother had taken a house in Harley Street and this was his home, though he visited Dublin in 1791 and again in 1792, to attend the session of Parliament and he stayed usually at Leinster House or in the family villa at Frescati in Blackrock. London however was the great attraction.

Lord Edward became a habitué of Devonshire House where his particular friend was his fellow-Irishman Richard Brinsley Sheridan. Lord Edward was in an embittered mood ; like his associates he was idle, he had now no regular occupation. He deemed his military career to have been blasted ; his love-affair in which he had been faithful and sincere, had ended on the lady's part in something like scorn. He therefore looked around for distraction and distraction could take only one form. Indeed he had confessed in a letter to his mother that when not otherwise occupied he must be making love. One might have thought that the Devonshire House environment would have suited his purpose admirably yet, whatever the entanglements there, it was elsewhere he gave his heart. The attraction was Elizabeth Linley, now aged thirty-five, a renowned beauty and noted also as a singer. She was the wife of Richard Brinsley Sheridan.

Twenty years earlier, Brinsley Sheridan, dramatist, theatre manager and politician, had come to London with a bride of such amazing beauty and accomplishment that she promptly became the talk of the town. Sheridan drifted into the theatrical business and being in desperate need of money wrote two comedies which have become part of English literature. He then turned manager, acquiring a major interest in Drury Lane, but whence he got the capital sum has never been satisfactorily explained. Nobody could unravel the bewildering tale of his borrowings, mortgages and counter-borrowings. Finally he turned politician, came to Parliament as Member for Stratford and soon was in the inner circle of the Whigs, the friend of Burke and Fox, the intimate friend of ' Prinny ', and a leading orator whose speeches all the ladies flocked to hear.

In all three spheres he had been an apparent success. He had come from Ireland penniless and unknown, son of a travelling actor and elocution teacher, he had prospered in love, he was a famous dramatist and some biographers call him a ' statesman.' He moved as an equal in the highest circles. Yet somehow there was a sense of unfulfilment. To begin with there is the long and mysterious tale of his debts, for behind the facade of success and brilliance there was ever the lurking shadow of the duns. These gentlemen indeed became such a permanent feature of the Sheridan landscape that the gay Richard Brinsley came to think of them as inevitable and to treat them as acquaintances. He would emerge in the morning, with new schemes and political manoeuvres, turning over in his mind some ornate period for a Commons debate or the Hastings trial. Coming down his doorsteps he would greet the duns with a wave and a smile. Sometimes the smile was a little weary. At a party in his house when the Prince of Wales exchanged doubtful jokes with Fox, Hare, Fitzpatrick or Lord Edward Fitzgerald, Sheridan in the midst of a good story would glance apprehensively through the window to see the duns outside. On one occasion he gave a great party at one of his country houses, (he kept two) ; a gathering on such a scale that the creditors decided to put forth a special effort. Sheridan had a difficult role that night, for he personally undertook to keep vigil outside and so keep the bailliffs out of the way of the guests. In the end as it was a cold night he invited the duns inside and having treated them well explained that he was short of servants. Two or three of them volunteered to act as servants and, some alterations in dress having been adjusted, proceeded to hand round the drinks.

It may be doubted if Sheridan himself ever understood his financial position. Certainly on the occasion of his second marriage he succeeded in convincing a prospective father-in-law, a grave Dean of Winchester, that he had an income of £10,000 a year, a feat which makes the authorship of the *School for Scandal* and the Begums of Oude speech look insignificant. It is a similar story in regard to his love-affairs : was he ever really in love with this beautiful young wife to whom so many other men had lost their hearts? He was unfaithful to her and glaringly so ; he carried on intrigues with titled ladies and with serving-maids, but he was never entirely neglectful of her. He always returned home—when they had a home—and rarely were there any scenes. There is little doubt that Elizabeth loved him sincerely ; indeed there was something odd about Sheridan that made many people love him ; yet for many years he and Elizabeth had ceased to live as man and wife.

III

Through the Whigs and the Devonshire House circle, Edward Fitzgerald became a close friend of Sheridan, and this led to a friendship with Elizabeth, a friendship which on both sides soon ripened into love. What sort of woman then was Elizabeth? Sheridan is usually described as having ' eloped ' with the beautiful singer from Bath, but elopement is scarcely the word; like most things in Sheridan's career this marriage affair presents complications. At the same time it had elements of farce which competed with the extravagant comedies put on under his management at Drury Lane.

Thomas Sheridan, Richard Brinsley's father, had come to anchor in Bath where he conducted an ' academy ' for elocution and deportment. He was reasonably prosperous. He had a family friend named Linley, a music teacher. Elizabeth the daughter was aged seventeen and already noted for her beauty and her voice. Already she had concert triumphs not only locally but even in London where she sang before Royalty. Naturally she had many suitors and after the eighteenth century pattern her father became anxious and wished to have her safely married. With some lack of humour a crusty and miserly old batchelor, named Long, then past fifty, was produced out of Wiltshire. Of course he was rich and he was reputed to be stingy but judging by the way he paid up afterwards he was evidently a man who wished at all costs for a quiet life.

Now why did the beautiful " nightingale of Bath " consider even for one moment a ridiculous, not to say outrageous, proposal like this? This is not the place to speculate on the reasons. Possibly at seventeen she knew no better than to regard marriage as an eighteenth century sale of a body ; perhaps she was unhappy, and most

women regard marriage—any sort of marriage—as a
suitable escape from present ills. From whatever reasons
she duly became engaged to old Long and her father was
anxious to hasten the wedding.

There are few things which will drive a young lady to
distraction like two or more suitors of equal eligibility.
The standard remedy is to resolve to get rid of them all.
In Elizabeth's case there was another gentleman named
Captain Matthews. (His title to the military rank has
been disputed.) He fancied himself a favoured lover
but Elizabeth makes out that his importunities drove her
to such distraction that she contemplated suicide. At all
events, it turned out there was the supreme obstacle that
he was already married. When Elizabeth discovered
this addition to her previous worries she declared that
she could bear things no longer. She confessed to her
great confidant Alicia, Richard Brinsley's sister that she
would either flee or kill herself. Sheridan himself who was
only twenty at the time was called in as confidant. Elizabeth said that she wished to fly to France and enter a convent, at least for a time, and there and then Richard Brinsley was constituted her ' protector ' and it was arranged
that in this chivalrous capacity he should accompany her.

The pair reached London and Dunkirk and here it
seems they went through some form of ceremony, procur-
ing a clergyman for the purpose ; but the marriage, if
such it was, was not consummated. Elizabeth retired to
her convent in Lille while Sheridan lived in a hotel.
There was the inevitable sequel. The lady's father,
indignant and worried, arrived. The couple were fetched
back to Bath but they did not represent themselves as man
and wife and the ceremony at Dunkirk was proved to be
invalid for non-compliance with the law. The next
episode was that Sheridan fought two duels with the discarded lover Matthews who had published some defama-
tory matter. Sheridan and Elizabeth took to meeting in

secret in defiance of a parental ban and they corresponded, not very warmly it must be confessed on Sheridan's part, and eventually they were married in April 1773 nearly a year after the Dunkirk escapade.

There are a number of things in this compressed tale which offend against probability. Sheridan if not deeply in love with Elizabeth Linley was kind and helpful during the troublesome Long and Matthews affair, but even then he was given to amorous flirtation. He had also some glimmerings of prudence. A boy like him, hanging about in Bath and dependent on his father, was in no position to marry, and it is not surprising that the parents objected. He did not intend to remain always in Bath and indeed in the restricted local society his talents had already attracted notice. He had great and vague ambitions. Most of all he must have felt—even then—the insistent artistic prompting ; within five years he was to write two immortal comedies and this creative urge goes ill with the restrictions of conventional marriage.

On the other hand there is no doubt that Elizabeth Linley was deeply, almost overwhelmingly, in love with him. Whether women possess that intuition to which they lay claim is debatable, but there is much evidence that young men of genius have attracted the interest of women for reasons wholly unconnected with worldly prospects or even physical attraction. Certainly Sheridan aged twenty had little obvious recommendations. Elizabeth's father thought him a ne'er-do-well, while to add to the confusion his daughter had other suitors. (During the interval after returning from Dunkirk she refused a baronet.) Yet she would consider no one but Sheridan, she would make any sacrifice to be his wife and to yield to him with that abandon which only a woman in love can feel. One would like to end the tale by remarking that they married and lived happily ever afterwards, but this unfortunately is not altogether the case.

Though she was courted and sought after and something of a celebrity, the nineteen year-old bride wished above all for a quiet and settled home. She considered that she possessed the essentials—she was married to Sheridan—but she yearned for many incidentals that Sheridan could not give and in the first enthusiasm of passion she did not advert to these. Sheridan was not an unkind man, but he could only be faithful in his fashion.

As the years went by she realised that the price paid for the glittering success was too great. And now at the age of thirty-seven she knew that she had not long to live. The seeds of consumption, the disease which imparted the ethereal beauty which inspired Reynolds to paint her as St. Cecilia, were present even before she left Bath. She had never wanted to be unfaithful, but now someone appeared who extended to her that quiet love which she had always desired. Here was love uncomplicated by ambitions and debts, untarnished by the intrigues of the Prince of Wales and his set and untroubled by endless chasing after other women. What could she owe to Sheridan who even at this time, after eighteen years of married life was having a scandalous love-affair with my Lady Duncannon? It is dangerous for a woman to rely on a man younger than herself and Lord Edward was eight years younger, yet his affection had a soothing quality which she had never hitherto experienced. She gave herself to him without regrets.

We can only speculate on the nature of Lord Edward's feelings for there are few details available. The affair seems to have passed more or less unnoticed. The Duchess of Leinster and the family were then living in Harley Street and they spent the time in a round of balls and dinner-parties varied with visits to Ireland and abroad, and with week-ends with Lord Henry and his wife then settled at Boyle Farm on the Thames opposite Hampton

Court. At least two of the daughters were fond of gossip and kept intermittent diaries, and they make no mention of brother Eddy's affair. But it is significant that, when the whole family left for Switzerland, Edward remained behind, being unable to separate from the dying Elizabeth. The family must therefore have been aware, but the Duchess loved her son so much that she took an indulgent view. Not so Ogilvie. Edward and he were good friends, and it speaks well for the gruff Scotsman that this respect and friendship grew. But Ogilvie did not like the company in which Edward was now mixing and he frequently complained in the strongest terms to the Duchess. She smiled the matter away and said that she believed all Edward's intentions were good, though she wished he were more moderate.

It may be doubted if he was much in love, although the helplessness of Elizabeth, the exhausting tales of neglect by Sheridan, and above all the imminence of death, roused all that was affectionate in his nature. Elizabeth spent much time at the hot wells in Bath, Lord Edward followed her there, and was present when she died in 1792. Not long before she died she gave birth to a daughter, and there is evidence that Lord Edward was the father of this child, and Elizabeth herself believed that he was.

While this was going on Sheridan was conducting a minor flirtation of his own. He was now involved with a sixteen-year old French girl of great beauty, with dark hair and eyes strangely reminiscent of Elizabeth. There was some mystery about this French girl. Meantime she recalled to the jaded Sheridan some of the romance of the days long ago in Bath and the early years of marriage. He took the young lady and her guardian to visit the ailing Elizabeth, and Elizabeth was favourably impressed. She told Eddy about the beautiful French refugee but Eddy was just a trifle bored, his entire interest for the moment being taken up with Elizabeth herself. She suggested that he should meet the new attraction, but Eddy replied banteringly that he was frightened off by the guardian, Madame de Genlis, who had a reputation for learning and had even written books, and Eddy made it clear that he could not abide learned ladies. So no meeting took place, and Elizabeth felt rather sorry. However much she loved Eddy, she realised that she was eight years older and that she had not long to live. She had all the unselfishness of a woman who had little to hope for, and she took the attitude that she would like Eddy to meet someone else. She had a poignant notion that when she was dead this young girl, with a beauty reminiscent of her own, would preserve her memory for Edward. She even said to him that if he were to marry she wished him to marry this French stranger. The girl's name was Pamela.

nine

I

THE reformist doctrines which Lord Edward heard constantly discussed at Devonshire House did not seem to go far enough. True, the Whig leaders gave some approval to the French Revolution, but there was always the suggestion of political scrambling for place. Lord Edward was interested in other things, radical theories which proposed the equality of man with man and the equal distribution of wealth. Governments, so far as they were tolerated at all, should be elected on manhood suffrage. Even his cousin Charles James Fox, Lord Edward found, had never thought of going as far as this—at least up to the present.

But there were other circles in London where there were no hesitations. It so happened that there was a small group which centred round Tom Paine, one of the most remarkable figures of the late eighteenth century. Since 1787 Paine had been in England, living in obscurity and frustration and amusing himself with scientific projects. His fortunes seemed at a low ebb. Son of a Norfolk Quaker, a staymaker by trade, Paine was born in 1737 and was intended also to be a staymaker, a trade he followed for some time. He afterwards became an exciseman but was dismissed from that office largely on account of what we would now call trade-union activities. At the

age of thirty-seven he found himself without any occupation and decided to emigrate to America where he arrived
just in time for the agitation that preceded the War of
Independence. In America Paine turned journalist, and
in a short time became a sort of official apologist and
pamphleteer for the insurgent colonists. There can be no
doubt that the help he gave was immense. His pamphlet
Common Sense aroused the greatest enthusiasm, indeed
some authorities consider that it was Paine, and not
others to whom the credit is usually given, who was the
chief architect of the new republic. Not only did he take
an active part in the campaigning, but also in the middle
of the war he crossed to France and there negotiated a
loan which ensured final victory. When victory did come
he was treated shabbily by the Americans. Of course he
had made enemies ; what man propounding his revolutionary doctrines would not ? Also, successful politicians did not like a man of Paine's stature so near the
throne ; his intellectual qualities might be a reflection
on their own mediocrity.

In the event Paine returned to England and for some
years lived a quiet life. But if existence in England was
static, there were certain tremendous events elsewhere
which excited him greatly. In 1789 the Bastille fell.
Still Paine held his peace. Then in 1790 there appeared
a work entitled *Reflections on the French Revolution* by
Edmund Burke.

Now it may be said that there are few books with a
reputation for greatness which will serve to exasperate a
modern reader like the *Reflections*. There, principles and
theories which have since been laughed out of existence
are served up as if they were immutable and self-evident
truths garnished in bombastic and ornate periods. Sentimental sympathy is invited for outworn institutions and
within these limits a system of ' regulated liberty ' is
devised by Burke. Paine set himself the congenial task

of demolishing Burke, and the task was relatively easy. In the *Rights of Man* he produced an eloquent statement of principles which went further than anything as yet seen in England. The average person accepted the platitudes of Burke as radical truths for the reason that no one had ever questioned them and men always tend to argue that things which are unquestioned are therefore unquestionable. In 1791 the *Rights of Man* was a phenomenal success. Fifty thousand copies were sold in Britain, and there were also French and American editions. Even the Tories were impressed, and Pitt, when importuned to take more effective steps at suppression, replied privately that he believed Paine's arguments were unanswerable.

In Ireland the book aroused the greatest enthusiasm amongst the Presbyterians in the North, particularly in Belfast, where French doctrines of liberty and equality were much in favour. But the *Rights of Man* circulated extensively through all the provinces and was read with interest by some literate Catholics. Indeed Tom Paine's book had no little influence in the final conversion of the United Irishmen from a reformist society into a revolutionary movement ; at a later date the United Directory had a plan to bring Paine over to Ireland but it did not materialise.

In the latter part of 1791 Paine was lodging in Marylebone, London, with an old friend named Thomas Rickman, and Rickman kept some notes of the friends and disciples who foregathered at the house. Amongst these names is that of Edward Fitzgerald. Paine visited France in June 1791, and before this he had lodgings in Islington, but the regular meeting place of the radical friends was eventually settled at the White Bear, Piccadilly, now the site of the Criterion Restaurant. The company was often a distinguished one, for Paine numbered amongst his friends Horne Tooke, Godwin of

Political Justice fame, Cartwright, Jebb, Romney the painter, Priestly and William Blake the poet. Lord Edward laid no claim to the intellectual accomplishments of the others, but he found the ideas discussed in this company very congenial and he reflected on the corrupt oligarchy which passed as a Government in Ireland and on how best the theories he heard discussed might be put into effect.

Lord Edward conceived an almost extravagant admiration for Paine. Paine was undoubtedly a great humanist, and there is no use—in this world—in professing liberal theories unless one is prepared to put them into practice in private life. He was then a kind man in small things, and one who practised that supreme form of charity the doing of good by stealth. He sent money secretly to needy people without disclosing the source ; afterwards in Paris he saved the lives of many English notables some of whom were his bitter enemies. Yet for all that he was not, at least at this period, an easy man to get on with. His opinions were often so subversive and advanced that they appeared dogmatic and, though he was an apostle of reason, he drew the line at trying to convince people who seemed incapable of thinking clearly. Moreover he had cause to feel excited. His writings in America had brought about independence and now his *Rights of Man* had, he believed, laid Burke in the dust, and seemed likely to bring about revolution even in England. A recent biographer remarks that at this period and for some time to come Paine was suffering from " cerebral excitement." All this, if true, was not apparent to Lord Edward, and to him Paine seemed to be the perfect man. Writing later from Paris he remarked that the more he saw of him " the more I like and respect him. I cannot express how kind he is to me ; there is a simplicity of manner, a goodness of heart and a strength of mind in him that I never knew a

man before possess." Such were the feelings of the
young man who was to carry some of Paine's teachings to
Ireland.

II

Meanwhile trouble was brewing for Paine in England.
Towards the end of 1791 a reactionary campaign was
whipped up ; the Government was really alarmed, all the
more as it was mooted that Paine was already engaged on
a sequel to the *Rights*, and it was decided that if possible
he must be got rid of.   To do this legally it was essential
first to arouse public feeling.   We shall see later how
this campaign got under way ;   before long Paine
(aided by William Blake) had to fly for his life and in
September 1792 he arrived in Calais having previously
been elected as a deputy to the French Convention.
Shortly afterwards he was followed to France by one of
his most ardent disciples.   Lord Edward Fitzgerald felt
that in Paris one could really see the principle of freedom
and equality in everyday practice.   The Revolution in
fact was now heading for its climax, though at the moment
there was a period of calm, and the great man Paine was
on the spot.

Lord Edward determined to go to Paris, but it was not
easy to think of a satisfactory excuse to give to his aristocratic London friends.   His association with Paine and
his circle was but little known and was overlooked as a
foible, for there were many cranky people throughout
England who professed admiration for Paine and the
Revolution.   Within the circle of his family there was
some misgiving, the Fitzgeralds were a devoted brood and
they kept no secrets from one another. At least one of
Lord Edward's sisters was fully aware of Eddy's dangerous associations.   His mother was worried ;   with a
woman's intuition she had sensed much, but she comforted

herself that his dabbling in strange cults was a passing phase, something to be expected in a young man who had been harshly used both in love and in his career. It would be banished, no doubt, only by marriage and a ' settling down '. The Duchess sighed frequently and wished that Eddy would find some girl who would make him a good wife and save him from the influence of undesirables like Paine. Little she thought that her prayer would be answered so soon, and that indirectly at least, Paine would be the instrument. Also it may be doubted if it was quite the answer she desired.

ten

I

AT this time there were many French emigrants in England. Some of them were *émigrés* in the accepted sense of that term; and there were some who had originally favoured the Revolution or had even been active in it, but, as happens in all revolutions, had fallen foul of the current party in power and had to fly. There were some who did not fit easily into either of these categories. Among these latter was Madame de Genlis.

Félicité Stéphanie, Countess de Genlis, now a handsome woman in early middle age, was by origin the daughter of a provincial landowner named Ducrest and she was born in Burgundy in 1746. At eighteen she married Count de Genlis, a colourless sort of man who afterwards succeeded to the Marquessate of Sillery. There were three children, two dying young, and Madame la Comtesse survived the other. An obscure and static existence was intolerable to Félicité de Genlis. She was a woman of considerable intelligence, with ideas on education much in advance of her time; and, as a minor novelist and writer on education, she achieved something like a European reputation. There is the fact that in 1785 Oxford University conferred on her a Doctor's degree, a remarkable distinction for a woman in the eighteenth century.

In 1770 she entered the service of the Duchess of Chartres, wife of the Duke of Chartres, cousin of the King. Chartres is better known as the Duke of Orleans and is famed as Philip Egalité of the Revolution, a title he assumed in 1792. Madame de Genlis was employed officially as tutor to the royal children, but her function extended much further than this. In this household, located chiefly at the Palais Royal, or at a country seat, she had a strange and adventurous life, but, on the whole, neither a happy nor a creditable existence. She was what we would call a woman of character, and in an unscrupulous and debauched environment it was difficult to preserve any principles. She has left a voluminous journal and correspondence. She had a flair for mendacity, but her lies are so transparent that they do not detract from the interest of the whole work.

She coveted the post of tutor, and at first sight it might seem that this was a small office for a woman of her ambition and capacity. Her real purpose, however, was to have an influential position at Court and if she could not have power in Versailles, she was content to officiate in the smaller theatre of the Palais Royal. In the pre-Revolution period the Palais Royal was the centre of much intrigue and counter-intrigue, and Orleans was dazzled with the vision that he might one day be put forward by the popular party as a democratic and constitutional King. His fate alas! was otherwise. But when the hour came he did not hesitate to vote for the death of his own cousin the King. His hopes had a belated fulfilment when his son the Citizen King Louis Philippe reigned for eighteen years, but by then Orleans was nearly forty years in the grave, having paid for his ambitions and vacillations by the guillotine.

Orleans was at one time an enormously wealthy man. When Madame de Genlis first came to the Palace he was still young, being in fact one year younger than herself,

and she was twenty-four. He had been three years married to Adelaide de Bourbon but already the lady Adelaide
was melancholy and disillusioned, for she had not yet
learned to grow hardened to infidelities. With a naivete
for which she can scarcely be pardoned, she had thought
that Orleans was a believer in monogamy. It may seem
surprising that a woman of the wit and sharpness of
Madame de Genlis could have been attracted by the
commonplace Orleans, but she had known sorrow and
poverty, and, what is worse than either, obscurity. She
realised the price to be paid to retain her influence and
status at Court. With whatever little enthusiasm, she
must yield to the embraces of her employer. And after
all, she calculated, he was a prince of the blood-royal,
and much therefore might be forgiven her. She was
efficient, and things could be managed efficiently; good
management covereth a multitude of sins.

We may pass over the various intrigues and quarrels
in the pre-Revolution Palais Royal in which she was
involved, and come to her visit to England. This
took place in 1785 to receive the Oxford degree. In
her capacity as governess she took with her two of
Orleans's daughters together with a dark-eyed little girl
of great beauty whose name was Pamela Sims and who
was described as the adopted daughter of Madame de
Genlis. The whole party kept up a considerable state
and lived in Orleans's great mansion in Portland Place,
where she entertained the Whig leaders and the Prince of
Wales. This gave Madame de Genlis an introduction
to the Devonshire House circle and there she was an
instant success. The ladies felt that she was no longer a
rival, while the men were relieved to meet for a change
a woman of some intelligence and experience, and one
whose life of effort made a sharp contrast to the languid
existence of their own ladies. She was received graciously

at Windsor, where Queen Charlotte was delighted to hold converse with the distinguished educationist.

Despite these impressive introductions the novelist Fanny Burney (who was keeping her journal at this time) had some doubts. Fanny was a prim little person, and expended much ingenuity in trying to form what she considered a " righteous opinion " of Madame de Genlis. " True, however, it is " she writes in her journal, " I believe her innocent of all crime but indiscretion, and of that I know not how to clear her, since to nothing softer can I attribute the grounds in which so much calumny has been raised. I imagine her to have fallen at an early and inexperienced period into designing and depraved hands, and not to have been able from cruel and distressed circumstances to give up the unworthy protection of a profligate patron though her continuing under it has stained her fame for evermore. . . " And there is more in the same vein, so it is evident that Madame de Genlis' reputation was not in Fanny Burney's estimation everything that one could desire. Another contemporary— and somewhat prejudiced—observer was Horace Walpole. Walpole disliked Rousseau, and he got it into his head that the educational theories of Madame de Genlis were intended to implement the doctrines of Rousseau; however, on meeting the lady he formed quite a favourable impression.

The adopted daughter was generally referred to as Pamela, but her real name was supposed to be Nancy Seymour or Sims. As is now generally admitted Pamela was the natural daughter of Madame de Genlis and her patron Philippe Egalité Duke of Orleans, but Madame steadily maintained the fiction that Pamels was an ' adopted ' daughter. Not only did she leave the child herself under that impression but she adhered to the story obstinately all her life, with such tenacity indeed that many people believed in it, almost to the present day. She had

to account somehow for Pamela, and she handed out a
tale which offends against common sense; it is difficult
to say why Madame de Genlis, a sophisticated woman,
expected anyone to believe it. The story invites ridicule
and must have prompted some of the pointed jests of
the experienced gentlemen in Devonshire House.

II

Madame, as we have noted, entered the Palais Royal
in 1770. In the Spring of 1776 she had a mysterious
illness and was ordered to the mineral-water town of
Spa in the Low Countries for a ' rest '. She remained
there for five months, and returned to the Palace none
the worse. The inference now is that, during this leave
of absence, Pamela was born, Orleans being the father.
On this reckoning Pamela would be three or four years
younger than her age as afterwards officially given.

It was essential to Madame's plans that there should
be no gossip or scandal. Not that another Orleans off-
spring could cause any comment but Madame had put
about such an atmosphere of prudery that it would be
fatal were it discovered that her adherance to the Orleans
faction was based on something more than political
loyalty. To gain this end she would go to any lengths,
and, suppressing her maternal instincts, she arranged with
a friendly secretary at the British Embassy that the child
should be shipped to England and there put out to a
foster mother at Christchurch in Hampshire. It is not
recorded that Madame de Genlis visited the child in
England, but when the child was a few years old she
arranged for her return to France. Madame was still
in the service of the Duke, but she lived mostly with her
charges in semi-retirement at the Convent of Bellechasse
in Paris, visiting the Palais Royal occasionally. Still, the
sudden presence of this beautiful little girl in the royal

establishment had to be explained. Madame de Genlis said that a child about their own age was required with whom the Duke's daughters could practise English, and that the Duke had commissioned one of his friends to procure him such a girl in England. The only corroborating factor of the adoption story is, (as stated in the Memoirs) that a formal procedure of legal adoption was in fact carried out and the Articles approved in Court by the English Chief Justice, Lord Mansfield. Henceforth Pamela was brought up within the Orleans household and educated by Madame de Genlis herself. She benefited to some extent from the love and tenderness of a mother but in after years Pamela bore little trace of having been tutored under the supervision of a learned theorist and authoress.

Pamela grew up to be a young lady of noted beauty but there is little on record to show that she was anything above the average in wit or intelligence. Her tastes were homely and unambitious. This is not surprising in one who witnessed the violent scenes of the Revolution and whose own life was more than once in danger. From her earliest years she had known unrest, intrigue, revolution and massacre, and she sighed for the quiet realities of home life. Her mother's career was one of endless preoccupation and worry. Frequently Pamela must have wondered at the purpose of it all and noticed that this political and dynastic turmoil had little relation to the quiet security for which a woman instinctively yearns.

III

The visit to England in 1785 was a short one, and Madame de Genlis did not come again until 1791. Meantime there had been great changes. The French Revolution had passed the first stages, and, more than ever, the Palais Royal became the centre of intrigue.

Madame de Genlis says that she was sent to England in
1791 by Orleans in charge of his daughter Princess Adelaide, accompanied by Pamela. She gives a variety of
explanations for this journey but the real reason was
that Orleans wished to send his daughter away for a time
from the atmosphere of revolutionary Paris. This, as it
turned out, was a dangerous move, for the dividing line
between an *émigré* and a ' tourist ' was a narrow one.
Also times had changed, and means were straitened.
There was no longer the great mansion in Portland Place,
and Madame de Genlis and her two charges stayed in a
small house off Park Lane. In the autumn she went to
Bath with the girls, and later she set up in a freakish
kind of establishment at Bury in Suffolk.

There were several mansions in England given up to
the accommodation of *émigrés* of the Revolution. These
little colonies of French nobility, together with their
camp-followers, gave great scope to the gossip-writers and
men of fashion; and equally great scandal to the more
prim ladies of the neighbourhood. At Juniper Hall, for
instance, near Leatherhead, there was a celebrated establishment which housed a number of persons including
Madame de Stael and—a great friend of Madame de
Genlis—Talleyrand.   Whereas, to put it charitably,
the conditions at Juniper Hall rather strained the conventions, the Bury Hall *menage* presided over by Madame
de Genlis was an affront to sanity. There were three
principals in the party, Madame de Genlis herself, the
Princess of Orleans and Pamela, yet the entire household
exceeded twenty; for a number of doubtful retainers of
Orleans made their way to Bury. Fanny Burney was
particularly shocked. " They have taken a house " she
writes " the master of which always dines with them,
though Mrs. Young says he is such a *low man* he should
not dine with her daughter. They form twenty with themselves and household. They keep a botanist, a chemist

and a natural historian always with them. They are supposed to have been common servants of the Duke of Orleans in former days, as they always walk behind the ladies when abroad; but to make amends in the new equalizing style, they all dine together at home. They have been to a Bury ball, and danced all night. Mademoiselle d'Orleans with anybody known or unknown. What a woeful change from that elegant, amiable, high-bred Madame de Genlis I knew six years ago—the apparent pattern of female perfection in manners, conversation and delicacy." Indeed poor Fanny's regrets did not even stop at that, for she notes with indignation that all Suffolk is full of " democrats ", among whom was the redoubtable Tom Paine " who herds with all the farmers that will receive him, and there propagates his pernicious doctrines."

Madame de Genlis may have been sent to England as guardian to Mademoiselle d'Orleans and Pamela; or, as she hints in her journal, there may have been other reasons for the visit. One purpose, however, she kept constantly in mind—she wished to have her daughter Pamela safely married to some Englishman of substance. One may guess that there would be no lack of candidates for the hand of the beautiful and mysterious young French girl, and indeed there was not—in a sense. There were plenty of younger sons, plenty of hangers-on, a sprinkling of rakes and bankrupts. There were quite a few eligible men, some no longer young, who professed undying love but reckoned that for the moment at any rate legal marriage was irrelevant. Madame de Genlis, mindful of her own troubled lifetime, was determined to be wary. And she realised that Pamela had certain disabilities ; she was dowerless, her birth was doubtful and she was infected with French ' democracy '. Nevertheless upon occasions the ambition of Madame de Genlis soared high, so that she had hopes of no less a person than Robert Stewart the future Viscount Castlereagh and Foreign Secretary, heir to the wealthy Marquis of Londonderry.

At length a gentleman appeared on the scene who seemed in many ways a strange choice. He was a very recent widower and rumour had it that he had been devoted to his deceased wife. This gentleman was none other than Richard Brinsley Sheridan. He had other drawbacks, he was now forty, was much the worse for wear, and his borrowings were famous and terrifying. He was still charmingly kind and patronising; he was a playwright of renown, and a prominent politician and orator; he was a friend of the Prince of Wales, and might at any moment become a Minister. Such qualities were not to be overlooked. In view of these allurements Madame de Genlis was prepared even to forget about the debts. It may be recalled, that Pamela was not yet seventeen. From the point of view of the beautiful young girl, Brinsley for all his kindness, may not have appeared as her precise idea of a hero of romance. His breath and his clothes frequently smelt of gin, and he had become a trifle swollen and gouty and occasionally rather stupefied. But he was willing to marry.

Like most incidents in Sheridan's life, his encounter with the *émigrés* was tangled and had its comic elements. As to what followed, different versions are given by interested parties. The first complication came as a rude and unexplained shock to Madame. For one reason or another Orleans got tired of the extended tour in England. No doubt he received hints that it did not suit his political colour, not did it look well in any guise that his daughter should be fraternising with notorious *émigrés* in England. As a matter of fact he was in serious trouble himself in many directions, amongst other things his fortune was gone. Having argued about the matter for some months with Madame de Genlis, he gave a peremptory order for return to France. He was in a position to enforce his decree for he informed Madame simply that there would be no more remittances. He gave as his excuse that new laws were pending against *émigrés*, which was true.

It seemed to Madame that this was a cruel stroke of fate—a hasty flight just when she was on the point of a favourable match for Pamela. She resolved to defy Orleans; even going to the length of detaining his daughter, although Orleans frantically explained that the penalty for the non-return of *émigrés* was death. There was a confused interchange; one account is given by Madame herself, but this is disbelieved by subsequent commentators. In her extremity, she appealed, through Sheridan, to Charles James Fox, himself overwhelmed with financial and gambling troubles. He could do nothing. She says that, being obliged to give up the house at Bury, Sheridan installed her and her charges at his country house at Isleworth, where they remained for a time. Towards the end of 1792, however, all three returned to France. Meantime Sheridan had proposed to Pamela and had, of course, been accepted. Madame sailed away comforted by the belief that the trip to England had not been entirely in vain, for, with an optimism which does her credit, she had faith in the constancy of Richard Brinsley Sheridan.

eleven

I

ON the death of Elizabeth Sheridan at Bath Lord Edward returned disconsolately to London. We have a glimpse of him in one of his mother's letters. " He is quite patient and even cheerful. Reads, looks after his plants in his windows, reflects a great deal upon everything, which makes his conversation quite charming. He is wonderfully sensible, has really a capacious mind—I wish it had some determined object. It is a pity it should run wild which it must do for want of it. I see it works up the abuses of government very much and most established customs. He is reading Milton's prose works. Travels he has given up ; they make him long to go away which he will not do while I live".

Some of the family were still in London, though his mother went on a visit to Ireland. He had nothing particular to do, but was in the mood for distraction, and was more and more drawn into the circle of Tom Paine. The great event of the year was the publication of the second instalment of Tom Paine's *Rights of Man*. The Government knew that this sequel was forthcoming and were alarmed accordingly. England, however, was the home of free speech and a free press; and the heart of old England was believed to be sound. But the ruling classes would have given almost any price to offset the impending calamity of a second *Rights of Man*, which was awaited not merely by a large body of workers but by a curiously-minded middle class and by the small coterie known as the intellectuals. The Government learned that Paine was attacking specific laws on the Statute Book. It was clear that something would have to be done and done quickly ; the terrifying example of France was there and the example of America where Paine's writings had been as damaging to British interests as the armies of Washington. Pitt was approached, he declared with something like impatience that there was nothing he could do as Paine, so far, had not broken the law. The usual suggestion was made that in that case the law could be altered. Pitt promised to look into the matter but it was urged on him with great earnestness that whatever the steps, they must be taken at once.

It was, then, a case of one impoverished and passionate writer against the vast resources of His Majesty's Government. If Pitt was willing but powerless, there were plenty of his followers who were equally willing and did not feel themselves at all powerless. They commenced a two-pointed plan of action ; firstly by some manner of means the publication of the second *Rights of Man* was to be prevented ; secondly there should be an organised campaign to work up feeling against the author. Paine, himself, when the atmosphere was right, should be prosecuted for treason and if at all possible, hanged. Neither of these benevolent projects presented great difficulties. Ignorant people are always more responsive to villification than to argument, and it is always easy to spread abuse. Paine's past was raked up. His personal history undoubtedly looked suspicious (he had been married twice and the second time had refused, on what we should say were ideological grounds, to consummate the marriage ; also he had been dismissed from the Customs.) The *Life of Paine* that appeared was, however, too obviously scurrilous to do much harm, and the campaigners had to think of something else. They approached the Mayors and Corporations, the country squires and the magistrates. These notables convened meetings and arranged lectures, passed loyal resolutions and sent up loyal addresses. Beer flowed freely at the lectures ; it was found easy to whip up resentment and enthusiasm amongst ignorant country-men and even easier amongst the half-starved town work-ers. The campaign became infectious. Soon the ' common people ' were holding meetings of their own and burning effigies of Paine ; the country gentlemen, finding that success exceeded expectations, entered in with a new zest. Paine was denounced as a traitorous adventurer, he had attacked the Fundamental Liberties of Englishmen and the Eternal Verities, and he had even questioned the existence of the God of the country squires. Resent-ment freshened to hysteria, hysteria as always produced a cry for blood and for a time Paine's life was in danger. He was threatened with dismemberment in the London streets.

This was all to the good, but the question still remained, what was to be done about the second *Rights of Man*? The proposed publisher was got at. It was suggested that he should buy up the copyright and then destroy the manuscript. Plenty of money was forthcoming, but Paine, of course, refused to sell. Then the Government resorted to a series of tricks which are a commentary on the conduct of Englishmen interested in Fundamental Rights, and on a Government with all its resources pitted against a solitary reformer. The authorities intimidated one publisher by threatening prosecution. Another publisher was found, and prevention of actual publication was seen to be impossible. In the end, the Government agents prevailed on a publisher to purloin the manuscript. That is to say, he was to feign friendship and at the same time fabricate delays in publication and meanwhile to pass on particulars of the contents. Then the extraordinary spectacle was witnessed of the Parliament of the Realm of Great Britain rushing through legislation so as to forestall criticism of laws in Tom Paine's *Rights of Man*. Eventually the second part appeared in 1792 and sold fifty thousand copies in a few weeks. The organised hostility did not, alas, give the Government a sense of security for clearly there were things in Paine's book which no amount of vilification, no appeal to ignorance and no invocation of the Almighty could gainsay. There were such proposals as universal suffrage, a just and merciful poor-law and criminal system, and the beginning of what we call a planned economy. Unfortunately Paine went a little too far—at least according to the laws of the day; the sale of the *Rights of Man* was stopped by Royal Proclamation, and eventually a warrant was procured and Paine had to fly for his life.

II

Lord Edward witnessed this persecution of one whom he admired so much in the silent aftermath of the death of Elizabeth Sheridan. Up to the middle of 1791 he was at Hot Wells near Bath but in the late summer he returned to London and was gathered up in the excitement surrounding the attempted publication. Lord Henry was still living on his estate at Boyle Farm, and Edward spent much of his time at this pleasant spot.

There were stirring events on the Continent too. In June 1791 the Royal Family had attempted to escape from France but were caught at Varennes and brought back; and now in 1792 the star of the Jacobins was in the ascendant and it was part of the Jacobin policy to have the King executed. The Girondists were losing ground daily. In September 1792 the Convention decreed the abolition of the monarchy in France, and in October a committee was set up to draft a new constitution. Meanwhile the Jacobins were steadily working up an agitation to bring the King to trial, hoping thereby to discredit the Girondists by making them appear as defenders of royalty. Eventually it was arranged that the King's trial would open in December. Several nations, including England, were threatening war or, as it was called, armed intervention. The stage indeed was set for great events, and it was at this juncture that Tom Paine arrived in Paris, having previously been elected a member of the Convention.

Lord Edward, left behind in London, could not long content himself as a mere spectator of the changes in France, and, besides, Paine was now there. His mother and most of his family were out of town so that he had not to employ deceptions to conceal his association with revolutionaries. Indeed in a letter to his mother, dated October, he makes merry on the French victories at the expense of the Prussian cavalry and says that cousin Charles Fox feels the same way. Nevertheless the family was getting decidedly worried and there were many confidential letters and conversations in the numerous tribe of aunts and cousins. Once more his mother sighed and once more she wished heartily that he would marry and settle as a somnolent country gentleman on his small Irish estate. She, knowing him better that most, was aware that he had strong domestic attachments and that at heart he loved the quiet and security of home.

But Lord Edward at the moment had other ideas. To go to Paris, and witness at first-hand the great events taking place, to see the theories of Rousseau in the practice of everyday politics, to enjoy the converse of the delectable Tom Paine, to hear the strains of *Ça Ira* and the tramp of the revolutionary armies—this was life. At home there was nothing but frustration, introspection and stagnation. The attractions of Paris were irresistible.

Hence, some weeks after the flight of Paine, Lord Edward arrived in Paris accompanied by two young men of the same way of thinking, Sir Robert Smythe and Hurford Stone. His stay was destined to be short but fateful, two events took place in that short period which formed a great dividing line in his life and career and which meant that now he must look only to the future. The past was no more.

twelve

I

SURROUNDED as he was by a circle of disapproving relatives, Lord Edward did the wise thing. He went to Paris abruptly, and at short notice, and only some of his sisters were aware of the trip. As for his mother he decided to present her, as it were, with a *fait accompli*. He wrote therefore in October from the Hotel de White in the Passage des Petits, saying simply that she would be surprised to hear from him at this address. Despite the events of this year and the one previous, Paris was strangely quiet, but Lord Edward had missed the September massacres only by a matter of weeks. Indeed quite a number of English travellers of the period commented on the calm, which to them seemed unnatural, prepared as they were by the hostile pamphlets and speeches in England.

Lord Edward does not hesitate to give his mother all the unpleasant news, breaking it as gently as possible. " I lodge with my friend Paine—we breakfast, dine and sup together. The more I see of his interior the more I like and respect him. I cannot express how kind he is to me ; there is a simplicity of manner, a goodness of heart and a strength of mind in him that I never knew a man before possess. I pass my time very pleasantly, read, walk and go quietly to the play. I have not been to see anyone." And in the same letter, giving exact particulars of his address, he blandly tells his mother that he is to be addressed as " *le Citoyen Edward Fitzgerald* ". Truly the Duchess must have regretted for the hundredth time the influence of that evil genius the odious Tom Paine on her darling and innocent boy. There was nothing, however, that she could do, and much worse was to come.

About a week or so later a short and interesting news-item appeared in the English newspapers. It may be as well to quote it in full :

" Paris, Nov. 19th. Yesterday the English arrived in Paris assembled at White's Hotel to celebrate the triumph of victories gained over their late invaders by the armies of France. Though the festival was intended to be purely British, the meeting was attended by citizens of various countries, by deputies of the Convention, by generals and other officers of the armies then stationed in or visiting Paris,—J. H. Stone in the chair.

" Among the toasts were : The armies of France, may the example of its citizen soldiers be followed by all enslaved countries, till tyrants and tyranny be extinct.

"An address proposed to the National Convention— Among several toasts proposed by the citizens Sir R. Smith and Lord E. Fitzgerald was the following : May the patriotic airs of the German Legion (Ça Ira, the Carmagnole, Marseillaise March etc.) soon become the favourite music of every army and may the soldier and the citizen join in the chorus.

" General Dillon proposed : The people of Ireland ; and may Government profit by the example of France and Reform prevent Revolution.

" Sir Robert Smith (*sic*) and Lord E. Fitzgerald renounced their titles; and a toast proposed by the former was drunk:—The speedy abolition of all hereditary titler and feudal distinctions."

" Paris 1792."

That was all, and it is a pity that we cannot overhear some of the comments amongst the relatives at home. If we are to judge by Lord Edward's next letter, his mother must have replied before the news-item appeared, for his letter makes no reference to the incident and we cannot but presume that the Duchess would expostulate with him on such a rash exhibition. Edward would have felt called upon to explain his conduct. Instead the Duchess wrote conveying what, one feels, were ironic congratulations on the success of the armies of his new friends the revolutionaries. Edward hastens to reply that she was quite right about his joy at the taking of Mons and the success of the battle of Jemappes and goes on to give what the Duchess thought a rather annoying if rapturous account of the celebrations of victory. She was reassured, however, by some further homely details but most of all by the news that he was to return the following week and confer with Ogilvie about getting his majority in the army, if, he added prophetically, he was not scratched out of the army by then. Finally he adds one little piece of information that looked quite harmless. " I dine to-day with Madame de Sillery."

II

During the previous year there had been much talk in London about Madame de Sillery (better known as Madame de Genlis) ; and Edward knew that his mother, who was surprisingly fond of reading, admired the writings of Madame, particularly the novels. Edward had avoided the lady when in England and, although his letter now states : " I dine with Madame de Sillery", it is scarcely necessary to add that it was not Madame who was the attraction.

When Madame de Genlis returned to France with her two charges she was joined by her husband de Sillery and the party went to Bellechasse, where they met Orleans. Madame de Genlis says that her intention was to deliver up Mlle. d'Orleans safely to her father and then she and Pamela were to return to England where, she did not doubt, the faithful Sheridan would be awaiting them impatiently. There was however, a change of plan. Orleans professed himself to be very distressed at the proposed laws relating to returned *émigrés* and had vainly pleaded with the Commune to relax them in favour of his daughter. He besought Madame de Genlis to take his daughter and Pamela to neutral territory, and in the meanwhile he would see what could be done about having an exception made in their case. After much bickering, this was the course agreed upon, and it was settled that the next day the party would set our for Belgium, Madame, however, having the ultimate resolve to return to England. This left them one night in Paris and they did what many people do in the circumstances, they went to the play.

The theatre was the Feydeau and the piece was an operette by Cherubini. Madame occupied a box with the two girls. It so happened that an adjacent box was occupied by Lord Edward Fitzgerald accompanied by Stone, who had presided at the patriotic dinner at the Hotel de White. Lord Edward caught sight of the girls in the other box and his attention was drawn by the strik-ing likeness of the profile of Pamela to that of Elizabeth Sheridan, a likeness often noted. He asked Stone the names of the neighbours and was startled when he heard them for he had gone out of his way to avoid Madame de Genlis in England and had heard queer stories of the relations of Sheridan and the young Pamela.

So this was the celebrated Pamela. He noted all those things which a man—instantly attracted—observes about a woman : the great mass of dark brown hair above a pale complexion, the interesting turn of cheek and chin, the shy and unaggressive manners, and the figure, small perhaps, but already voluptuous. When the girl turned full face he noted the dark southern eyes and the wide sensual mouth and he may have noted that the face was not so long and pointed as that of Elizabeth Sheridan. At this point he recalled with a beating of the heart the words of Elizabeth as he gazed on Pamela's portrait, when she hoped that if he married after her death it would be a girl like her. He hastily recalled the jumble of all he had heard about Pamela. There was the lure of her mysterious and glamourous origin. Was she not, after all, a Bourbon? Lord Edward, one fears, did not give much attention to what remained of Cherubini's musical piece.

The Paris of the period was a place where men bent on action acted quickly. Stone was an acquaintance of Madame de Genlis, and Fitzgerald requested that he take him round to the box and introduce him. This was easily arranged, and Madame de Genlis received them graciously. But when she saw the look in Fitzgerald's eyes (his features were such that it was easy to read his feelings) the polite smile faded momentarily and gave way in turn to a look of deep interest which all her acknowledged powers of dissimulation were unable to control. She knew Lord Edward by repute. She had frequently spoken about him to Charles James Fox. She had met some of his cousins and many of his acquaintances at Devonshire House. She had heard frequent awed whispers—particularly amongst the ladies at Devonshire House—about his revolutionary views. It may be that some of the relatives had implored her, if the opportunity ever came her way, to use her influence to preserve him from all these dangerous contacts.

These things passed tumultuously through the mind of Madame de Genlis, yet they were but fleeting considerations. Being a woman, and more than that, a mother with a marriageable daughter in dangerous surroundings, she could only think of Fitzgerald as an eligible suitor. His family could rival that of the Bourbons themselves. He was the brother of the premier Irish Duke, he was well provided for, he was the nephew of Richmond and the cousin of the great Charles James Fox. He was an affectionate son and she recalled that an affectionate son usually makes a good husband. He had a high reputation for amiability and generosity—indeed his contact with revolutionary politics was directly against self-interest and family convention. By doing nothing save to take things as they were he could look forward to a life of elegance and ease. His splendid connections, if only he would use them in the right way and be done with these subversive activities, could procure him any advancement he pleased and she had heard rumours that William Pitt himself had already offered him a command in the Spanish war. This woman of the world accustomed to quick estimates of difficult and even dangerous situations passed everything in review ; for once her poise nearly gave way and she had to simulate indifference. It is said that a woman always knows when a man is in love with her. One thing seems certain, a match-making mamma will always perceive when a man is in love with her daughter. One glance at the features of Lord Edward as he conversed with Pamela told her that he had fallen in love at first sight.

III

The meeting, however, was a short one, there were many other things to be considered. Orleans had been allowed to keep his daughter only twenty-four hours within the realm and to-morrow she, Pamela and Madame de Genlis must set out for Belgium. There was to be a further discussion *en route* at Rancy, and Madame invited

Lord Edward to dinner there the following evening.
Lord Edward gladly accepted, and next day, before
setting out, he wrote to his mother a sober letter in
view of the circumstances.

The proceedings at Rancy were eventful. The Marquis
de Sillery was on the scene, and again there were long
discussions—not very friendly ones—between Madame
de Genlis the Duke of Orleans and de Sillery. There was
much to be settled, for Orleans had now committed himself to the Jacobins and Madame's dreams of an Orleans
dynasty seemed about to be realised—not, however, in the
way she intended. Meanwhile Pamela and Lord Edward
were walking in the garden in the dusk of a mild winter's
day. Madame de Genlis after the lapse of a day, had
already taken the betrothal almost for granted, and to-
morrow the journey was to be continued to Tournai. Lord
Edward therefore lost no time. That evening after dinner
he told Madame that he had proposed to Pamela and had
been accepted provisionally, and he now sought her
consent. We can picture Madame as being embarrassed
and as saying the usual things on such occasions. As
mentioned in her memoirs she raised the question of the
consent of Lord Edward's mother, but Lord Edward's
biographer, Thomas Moore, thought that the Duchess
did not hear of the wedding until it had taken place, or at
least until a few days before ; and he quotes a letter from
Lord Edward thanking the Duchess warmly for her bless-
ing on the union. Moore was inaccurate about this, for
immediately after the departure of the travellers to
Tournai Lord Edward took the packet to England to
visit his mother, who was then staying at Turnbridge Well.

There may be some curiosity as to Pamela's feelings in
this whole affair. She was well schooled to the view, then
quite common, that a fortunate marriage was something
of an achievement. It would extricate her from a dubious
position and from the turmoil of revolutionary Paris.

At the moment her status was that of a returned *émigré* awaiting the uncertainty of the law, and already the outlook was unfavourable. She had no fortune and no prospects; and we can never be sure whether she believed the story of Madame de Genlis that she was merely an adopted daughter, and that she was in reality Nancy Sims. Many years afterwards, when she was a middle-aged woman, she freely acknowledged that she was the daughter of Madame de Genlis and Orleans. As for love, if love coincided with a suitable marriage, it was all to the good; but the important thing was the marriage. Pamela felt that against a background of security and domestic peace love was sure to come, and to this end she would have dutifully married Brinsley Sheridan even though he was battered and impecunious and notoriously fickle, and despite the fact that he was twenty years or more her senior, and had a grown-up son.

But of course the unlucky Sheridan was instantly forgotten, not only by Pamela, but also, rather unblushingly, by Madame herself. That worthy was not perturbed, soon afterwards he found solace in a marriage with the twenty-year-old daughter of the Dean of Winchester. Contrasted with Sheridan, it seemed to Pamela that fate had raised up not only a suitable husband but also a very hero of romance. There was hardly a single quality which Madame or Pamela desired which Lord Edward did not possess. He was young, only twenty nine, a mere ten years older than Pamela if we are to accept Madame's version of her age. From the younger woman's viewpoint his person was attractive. The features were frank if not intellectual and over them there was a suggestion of kindliness and affection. His manner was easy, almost charming, and above all there were no complexities in his character.

Madame thought about his worldly prospects. He shared an admiration for Rousseau with Pamela herself, this was no defect ; perhaps it was merely the enthusiasm of youth. His political views, if not very clearly defined, were what we should now call definitely left-wing, but he was not committed to any dangerous association, and Madame reflected that in England it was always difficult for a man to make trouble for himself by being involved with the left ; Tom Paine's case was merely an exception. As for Ireland, Madame never thought of that country at all. She had heard little about Ireland and she seldom thought of Lord Edward in connection with it. Finally she shared with the Duchess of Leinster the belief that under the benign influence of marriage these disturbing things would gradually be forgotten. Most idealism gives way to respectability, independence gives way to sullen acquiescence, for nearly all men come to see that nothing they can do will alter the general pattern of affairs.

On his side Lord Edward—ever given to instant and complete surrender—was passionately in love. Moreover he was conscious that for the first time there were none of the difficulties that had blighted his previous affairs. Here was a new and intoxicating joy. The mother in the case was compliant. If she was enthusiastic she succeeded in concealing it from Lord Edward. He found it a great relief that his being a younger son was scarcely a matter of comment. In this harmonious atmosphere details of the marriage were arranged with all the dispatch of a fairytale romance ; Madame and her charges continued their journey to Tournai, while Lord Edward, in a high state of excitement, set out for England to see his mother and tell the great news to the family. There was but little time; it was already late November, and he was to return to France for the wedding which was to take place if possible before Christmas.

IV

Lord Edward hastened to Maidstone and arrived in an exuberant mood, but it is safe to say that the Duchess did not altogether share his enthusiasm. Anxious as she was to have dear Eddy married, Pamela was not by any means the kind of bride she had in mind. She wished for the daughter of a prominent Irish or English landowner and a member of the peerage, a girl of conservative upbringing whose views she hoped would be shared by Eddy. More than that she would have insisted on an adequate settlement. Eddy was not well provided for, and, up to the present at any rate, his tastes and way of life, if not exactly extravagant, were restless and expensive. She listened therefore with some gravity while Eddy gave her a lover's description and attempted to tell her about Pamela. His task was not easy. Pamela went by different names, and one of them, Nancy Sims, was not a very attractive one. Also it was difficult to say precisely who she was; but she was the adopted daughter of the celebrated Madame de Genlis. The Duchess inclined her head and with a half-smile steered the conversation away from this embarrassing subject. Fortunately she had a high opinion of Madame de Genlis. It might be that Madame had been for a time the mistress of Orleans; such a relationship was not uncommon in higher society, and the Duchess was well accustomed to the complicated amours of the Devonshire and Holland House circles, while herself the most virtuous of matrons. She recalled the spiteful gossip that had followed her own union with Ogilvie, a marriage which in the event had proved a great happiness to all concerned. She was a woman who had learned the supreme wisdom of not attempting to interfere with other peoples' lives. All things considered, matters could be worse.

It is never wise to give advice, but one can always tender the benefit of experience. There was therefore one unromantic matter to which the Duchess adverted. This was the financial aspect. Lord Edward had given little, if any, thought to this and like many young lovers was not disposed to concentrate on any serious reckoning. Nevertheless the Duchess saw that, however unwillingly, the matter must be considered. Edward's provision under the family settlement was inadequate, as it amounted only to about £800 a year in the existing currency. Also he had no settled home and might have to buy a house. Then there was the cost of living. The Duchess recalled with satisfaction that Eddy was not dissipated; he was not a gambler like cousin Charles Fox, nor encumbered with mysterious debts like Sheridan ; but she knew that his present manner of living could not be maintained with a wife and family on his income. It seemed to Eddy that this was not immediately pressing, and the Duchess left it at that.

Eddy then went to London to see his sister Lady Sophia who was staying at the family home in Harley Street. This little lady differed rather from all the other members of the Fitzgerald family ; she was small and rather plain, she was affectionate but fond of solitude, and she never got on really well in the family circle. In time she went to live in a cottage near Thames Ditton where she lived out a long and fairly happy life, busy with her garden and correspondence, helping in the village and occupied with all the other small interests of the contented spinster. She was Eddy's favourite sister and to her belongs the distinction of caring for his children after his death.

Sophia fortunately kept a journal and from time to time recorded in an unaffected way events which interested her. The engagement of Eddy to Pamela Seymour was of course an outstanding event and Sophia confesses herself not merely surprised but highly amused, " There was " she writes " something very Odd and extraordinary in the Idea of his meeting with a young person that was educated by Madame de Sillery, whom we used to laugh at formerly and thought her *Plans d' Education* all perfect nonsense and delighted in worrying my mother (who admires all her writings in the greatest degree) by telling her, her charming Madame de Genlis tho' she wrote books, her own character was not free from censure, and that she was imagined to have been the Duke of Orleans' Mistress". Sophia was not sure if this were true but as to the engagement she goes on to say " After my first surprise was over the Idea of his going to be married did divert me so, I did nothing but laugh every time I thought of it. At the same time I was delighted to hear it and we spent a very comfortable Evening, he and I, talking it all over. He staid but three days in London and set off immediately for Tournai." and she says " I do hope and trust Dearest Edward has met with a Woman that will fix him at last and likely to make him happy the remainder of his life." And with this pious wish behind him Edward set out for Tournai.

V

While the joyful anticipation and preparations went on in the household at Tournai, there were other happenings of a less pleasant, if scarcely less fateful, nature elsewhere. We may recall the dinner which Lord Edward attended in Paris to celebrate the republican victories. In the eighteenth century there seems to have been a craze for the celebration of revolutionary events by the holding of dinner-parties. Dinners took place on different occasions in Ireland, in England and in France, and they all followed the same formula. Men ate and conversed and drank a great measure of wine ; the wine encouraged enthusiasm and in an atmosphere where all was unanimity gentlemen made speeches and used extreme words. The main result of these dinner-parties was to draw the attention of government agents. At the Paris dinner in November strange toasts were honoured, and the citizen Edward Fitzgerald had publicly renounced his title of honour and pledged support to the Revolution.

This was a fairly serious avowal for one in his position: an officer in His Majesty's Army, and the Paris declaration did not go unnoticed. One may doubt if the rather provocative toasts represented the sober views of all who attended, but if they did, the cause was not well served by thus being flaunted in public. A brief account with names, had appeared in the English press and the sequel was swift and drastic. Lord Edward, with three others, was dismissed His Majesty's Service. No opportunity was given the parties of making representations and no formal charge was ever preferred. Whatever we may now think of army officers being identified with celebrations glorifying the French Revolution, the fact that they were punished without a chance to defend themselves and even without a formal charge is contrary to the spirit of English liberties, and the Courts of Justice, if they could have been invoked, would have pronounced that such procedure offended against natural justice. The young men never knew with what crime, if any, they were charged and it does not appear from the newspaper report that any known offence was committed. Charles James Fox raised the matter in the House when speaking on a motion of the Secretary of War but nothing further was done or could be done.

Coinciding as it did with all the excitement of preparations for marriage the blow to Lord Edward, for the moment, was softened. But it would be a mistake to think that it did not affect him deeply. There are single incidents in life which alter the whole cast of mind ; it is said that time heals wounds, which is true provided one is speaking only of the initial pain. There is much evidence that this is what happened to Fitzgerald. Nothing leaves a more serious or lasting effect than an injustice deliberately perpetrated and sustained under the guise of legality, because it saps the reliance of the individual in standards which he has been taught to accept. Henceforth, therefore, he must measure conduct by new and unknown criteria and seek what Francis Bacon called "wild justice" meaning justice outside the ordinary channels of the law. We may be disposed to ask what after all was a paltry commission in the army? Yet it so happens that these things may be almost as dear as life itself to the individual concerned and we have no right to judge, that is to say apply our own standards of value. Certainly the dismissal had a profound effect on Lord Edward, whose whole ambition was bound up with an army career. Writing many years after his death his mother dates all those extreme views which led to the final tragedy from the time of his dismissal from the army. There were many evil stories going the rounds in London at this time relating to Lord Edward and his revolutionary views and Lady Sophia confessed herself shocked at the malice of some of them. As to the removal from the army list she hinted at some mysterious person who could have saved the situation. This was probably Richmond. Richmond, however, had become quite estranged from Edward and refused to move. Lady Sophia commented " What a shameful piece of business this was too," (the dismissal from the army) " and when one recollects that there is a *person* in whose power it was to prevent their doing it, it makes the circumstances still more aggravating."

It is possible that Lord Edward did not hear the bad news till just on the eve of the marriage ; certainly he did not know of it when making the hurried visit to his mother and Lady Sophia. Meantime in Tournai the preparations had been pushed ahead and the marriage took place on the 27th December 1792. There was a civil contract followed by a religious ceremony in the Church of St. Quentin. The civil contract is interesting for the details it gives of the birth and parentage of Pamela, publicly recording the story of the adoption, and interesting also for the array of well-known names appended as witnesses. The contract describes Pamela as Citizeness Anne Caroline Stephanie Sims, native of Fogo, Newfoundland, daughter of Guillaume de Brixey and Mary Sims, and the signatories include not only Philippe Egalité, who signs as such, but also a certain L. Philippe Egalité who was afterwards to reign as Louis Philippe, King of the French.

The Tournai register described Pamela as daughter of William Berkley but this has been explained as a clerical error. Hitherto Madame de Genlis had given ' Seymour ' as the name of Pamela's father but this aristocratic sounding name was abandoned now. Doubts as to Pamela's acceptance by the clannish Fitzgerald family were quickly set at rest ; Pamela pleased everyone by her beauty and simplicity. Sophia records in her diary that " Pamela was besides being very handsome. . . uncommonly sensible and agreeable, very pretty, with the most engaging pleasing manner I ever saw, and very much accomplished. They spent a fortnight with us in London before they went to Ireland where they are now."

thirteen

I

LORD EDWARD was still a member of the Irish Parliament, and, although he had not lived permanently in Ireland for many years past, and the entire family, except Leinster, lived in England, he felt that Ireland was his real home. In any case he had a duty to attend the session, and on January 25th 1793 he and Pamela arrived in Dublin. The first task for newly-married folk is to find a home. From the woman's point of view, marriage without the background of a home cannot be called marriage at all, and in Pamela's case this consideration was especially strong. Lord Edward had no home of his own in Ireland, and the problem of securing one was to exercise their minds for nearly a year. Eighteenth-century Dublin it seems was not altogether dissimilar from the Dublin of to-day.

For the moment, they put up in the spacious apartments of Leinster House, the town residence of the Duke. Leinster lived chiefly in the country, and Leinster House was to remain a Dublin headquarters for Lord Edward and his wife until the end. Also they had the use of ample alternative accommodation. There was the villa at Frescati, originally built at great expense by the first Duke and now greatly extended. It was a sort of dower house for the Duchess, but Ogilvie was always endeavouring

K

to let it; meanwhile when the Spring came Edward and his wife could live there while they were still looking round for a place. They had many invitations. Lord Edward's aunt, Lady Louisa Conolly, was the châtelaine of Castletown near Celbridge, said to be the largest country-house in Ireland, and Lord and Lady Edward spent much of their time there. Edward then considered renting a house in County Wicklow as he longed for country life combined with mountain and sea.

Dublin at that time ranked second only to London in elegance and fashion. Privilege was confined to a relatively narrow circle, and where interests are limited people inevitably turn to gossip. So it was in Dublin, and to judge by the letters and journals that have come down to us the ladies of Dublin were great gossips. A woman's life could be dreary in these great country mansions and almost equally monotonous in the great town houses. Besides it was an insanitary age. There was much indifferent health among the ladies, there is continual reference in the memoirs to colics, faintings, days in bed and complaints which seem mysterious to us now. It was all very well for the men, they made sure to offset the boredom of life by the excitements of fighting and gambling and heavy drinking. The ladies' journals constantly refer to men having arrived ' drunk ' and even the exceptional Lord Edward does not escape the reference. He himself writing to his sister Sophia admits that he had attended a ' Patriotick Dinner ' where he had got stupid and drunk and the following day his aunt, Lady Sarah Napier, then staying in the Blackrock neighbourhood, takes up the tale. Lady Sarah, it may be recalled, was once deemed the most beautiful woman in London and had refused the hand of George III or, as is claimed, she was intimidated by the Tories on account of her powerful Whig connections. In Ireland, as a matron, it is evident that she had her own small share of troubles. Writing to

Sophia, Lady Sarah says " I must now give you an account of my distresses since you went. On Thursday I went to Lady Jameson's and to Mrs. Meynell's, which, as it was *hot*, certainly did fatigue me a little, but I was sure to make up for it on a quiet evening and early going to bed. Mr. Ogilvie sat and chatted with me till 10, and at 11, I was preparing to go to bed, when in walks Mr. Napier, *drunk as an owl*, with 2 *Colonels*, whom I had never seen, and Edward as *Drunk* as his good uncle. ' Sarah, I have brought these gentlemen to supper : give us some bread and cheese.' You have no idea of my *blank face*, for one of the Footmen was gone to bed very ill ; I did not know what there was in the House, or if the Cook was up to dress it, and I *saw* that Donny was not in a way to understand reason on any subject. However, after I had recovered my surprise, I put the best face I could on it, and we managed *tant bien que mal*, and my only reason for conversation was worrying Eddy about his love of his wine, for the two Colonels would not utter for fear of exposing themselves. I gave them strong beer to make them more drunk that they might *go* the sooner ; as for Eddy, he *stuffed* and he *drank comme quatre*, and was my only comfort, for Mr. N. was *wise and stupid*. At last Eddy went, and I retired at one o'clock to bed, being too much worried by this supper to sleep. At 3 Mr. Napier came up and showed me a Boat close to the shore, where he and MacDonald had discovered thieves in, and they had been lying out on the Terrace with Pistols in case the thieves stirred. This pretty piece of intelligence kept me *en l'air* for 2 hours more : the Boat went off, and we were safe for that night. Well, on Saturday *I determined to have a good night's rest*, when behold at 12 o'clock Mr. N. was seized with the gout in his stomach worse than ever. The things he took added to the Pain, and by 2 o'clock he was convulsed and could neither see nor hear. I sent for Mr. Welch, and was happily relieved from my terror by his assuring me all danger was over, that it was not inflammation in the Bowels as I thought it, but a bilious colic, which Castor Oil would remove : it did so at the end of 12 hours and left him so weak and so yellow that he will not be himself this week I fear. You may guess a night of horror and running up and down-stairs was not very likely to *rest* me ; however, I have since made up all my fatigues by quiet and sleep, and am now quite well again."

II

In a gossipy city the arrival of Lord Edward with a French bride—said to be the daughter of the Duke of Orleans—was a matter of great interest to the ladies. There was a undeclared covenant to be hostile to Pamela. Lady Sophia loyally accounts for this by saying that many of these ladies had been in love with Lord Edward, and, not having succeeded in marrying him they were annoyed that he took a bride so different from themselves. Though the hostility never amounted to more than feminine jealousy combined with curiosity, the ladies whispered strange and malicious stories. Pamela was supposed to possess a handkerchief dipped in the blood of some of the French aristocrats. It was rumoured that she wore the French cap of liberty, that she hummed revolutionary hymns and that Lord Edward wore a green neckerchief, and that in general she possessed an evil influence over him. There was no dispute about her origin. The story that she was the adopted daughter of Madame de Genlis was scarcely mentioned; and when a current news-sheet in Dublin described her as the daughter of Orleans no steps were taken to contradict it. With the Fitzgerald family Pamela was a favourite, for she had a gay and unaffected nature; she was liked by the Duchess and the family in London, and the Lady Sarah was so much taken that, in her own words, she found it difficult to believe that she could be the daughter of " that vile Egalité."

With the men Pamela was a great success and the gallants did not worry in the least about her alleged humming of revolutionary songs. She was young, certainly not more than nineteen, though there is evidence that her age at this time was only sixteen. She was fond of dancing and was always eager to go to a rout. The winter of 1792-3 was a long succession of assemblies in Dublin; Pamela went to them all, and brought a slightly reluctant Lord Edward with her. She was courted and admired, even by such conservatives as Viscount Castlereagh ; life was gay and happy and she wisely ignored the cat-like glances of the young ladies.

As always there were one or two worries in the immediate circle of her life. She had a horror and a hatred of revolutionary intrigue, of riots, shootings and executions. In France she had never known any other sort of life, nothing else was of interest in the Palais Royal or even in Bellechasse. As for Ireland—she knew nothing of that country : it was an island, a part of England as it were, that lay more to the west. To go and live there would at least have one merit ; it was unlikely that the political turmoil which seemed to be an inevitable part of life in France could have penetrated to that remote and tranquil island. With something of dismay she discovered that this was not the case at all. Things had been bad enough in France but they seemed almost as bad in Ireland, if anything a little worse. Almost from the day of her arrival there were strange and noisy scenes in Parliament, while throughout the country there was never-ending talk of secret societies of which she knew little as yet. She learned with alarm that there were plots for an armed rebellion, even for invasion by the French.

III

Lord Edward had arrived in Dublin at a time of grave
crisis, for Lecky describes the session of Parliament
which opened in January 1793 as one of the most important ever held by an Irish Parliament.   Once again external
events affected Irish government policy.   Louis XVI was
executed on January 21st 1793 and the Jacobins were in
power ;   the British Government was alarmed about
conditions in Ireland and the fear amounted almost to
panic.   The Cabinet would tolerate no more trifling and,
as we have seen, a peremptory direction was sent to the
Castle that full-scale Catholic relief was to be included
in the programme for the present session.   Only a year
previously the Government, blind to the dangers, had
turned down this request, though a truncated measure
known as Langrishe's Act had been passed.   Now there
were no half-measures.   If the matter was to be dealt
with at all then it must be done adequately.   Upon this
Pitt and his Cabinet were adamant.

But the British Government did not appreciate that
there were other currents then moving in Ireland.   These
movements went far beyond the Catholic demands, and
the effect was that the Catholics were despised for their
subservience.   In Ulster the revolutionary ferment was
most evident, and there in July 1792 the anniversary of
the French Revolution was celebrated with a procession,
a festival and the inevitable dinner.   It is significant that
Catholic delegates from the South were present, rather
to the annoyance of the Dublin Catholic leaders.   Earlier
a message of congratulation had been sent to the French
National Assembly and a cordial reply received.   If
agitation had stopped short at dinners and addresses of
congratulation the Government might have afforded to
leave matters alone—there was little to be feared now that
the kingdom was at war, and repressive wartime measures

could be put into operation. But behind the demonstration there was the threat of the United Irishmen and the remnants of the armed Volunteers, for it was proposed that the Volunteers should be revived on the French model of the 'National Guard'. Many of the old Volunteers would have nothing to do with this development, and the main force had long been disbanded; on the other hand there were many new recruits, including Catholics, and in Dublin a battalion of this new National Guard was formed. The Government had to act, it was decided that all these armed bodies should be suppressed, and to comply with the existing law it was necessary that this suppression should be done by way of parliamentary Address.

On the motion for the Address Lord Edward figured in a scene. Waiting until the other Opposition speakers were finished he declared passionately " Sir, I give my most hearty disapprobation to this Address, for I do think that the Lord Lieutenant and the majority of this House are the worst subjects the King has."

This was followed by a scene of confusion and the House was cleared. Complying with entreaties from his friends, Lord Edward purported to give an apology which if correctly reported is not without a certain touch of humour. " I am accused " he said " of having declared that I think the Lord Lieutenant and the majority of this House are the worst subjects the King has ; I said so, 'tis true, and I'm sorry for it." This did not sound to the House as being altogether penitent, and a resolution was passed " That the excuse offered by the Right Hon. Edward Fitzgerald, commonly called Lord Edward Fitzgerald, for the said words so spoken is unsatisfactory and insufficient ", and he was ordered to appear at the Bar of the House on the following day. Accordingly he appeared at the Bar in custody and gave some words of explanation which are not reported, but a minority of fifty-five voted against accepting it. Lecky remarks of the incident that it is important as showing that alone in the Commons Lord Edward represented ideas which were spreading throughout the country.

The session drew to a close. In addition to the Catholic Relief Act it was remarkable for one other Statute which was to prove an irritant to Nationalist movements for the next two generations. This was the Convention Act. The Government had witnessed the great moral force of national conventions, more representative by far than Parliament itself and expressive of the will of the people. The Dungannon Convention had preceded independence in 1782, and recently the Catholic Convention had led the way to the Relief Act. Above all there was the example of the French Assembly on which these Irish Conventions were modelled. It was rumoured that a great National Convention, chosen on a representative basis and consisting of persons who shared the views of the United Irishmen and other revolutionary bodies, was to be held in Athlone, a town situated in the centre of Ireland. A Bill was passed making such gatherings illegal. Once again Lord Edward was in opposition. The erstwhile confidant of Tom Paine, as he sat on the Opposition benches, noting the cynical corruption opposite and the futile efforts of the Opposition, reflected that this so-called Parliament was merely the instrument of oppression and that it was time it was swept away altogether and replaced by an Irish assembly based on universal suffrage. In such an assembly the voice of the common people would inaugurate the new era of liberty and equality. This was the " great objective " to which he referred in his letter written years previously from Canada.

IV

There was still the personal problem of where to live. Lord Edward found the rooms of Leinster House unbearable. He records in a letter to his mother that

a young country maid who had come as a servant was
almost driven out of her wits by the gloom, and had
stayed only a few days. Carton, the country mansion
with its two thousand acres of parkland, was in no better
case, and the effect it had on Lord Edward has already
been recorded. Besides there was Pamela's insatiable
appetite for dancing, and after a trying day in the House,
usually spent by Lord Edward in smothering his anger,
one can appreciate that he was in no mood to face the
civilities of the dances, and he may have found it difficult
to be civil to Castlereagh and the other gentlemen attracted
by the beauty of Pamela. There is however no evidence
that her interest in others ever went further than a gay
and encouraging smile ; to the end she was a loyal
and devoted wife and Lord Edward was a happy
man.

In April they removed to Frescati as a temporary
home. Both Lord Edward and Pamela were delighted
with the freshness of the Spring season and he wrote
enthusiastic accounts to his mother. Here also there was
an extra occasion for joy when Pamela discovered that
she was pregnant. The negotiations for a permanent
home went on. He desired nothing more than a moderate
country residence where he and his wife could savour the
joys of early married life. He was much attached to
Frescati, and was loath to move; and moreover a baby
was on the way. There was a lodge at Carton which was
at his disposal but he wished to be as far from Carton as
was convenient. He then thought of settling in Co.
Wicklow near to the landed family of the Tighes with
whose younger sons he was friendly. He liked the Co.
Wicklow; it contrasted favourably with the featureless
expanse of Co. Kildare, and in a letter he says that he
wants to live amidst the mountains and near the sea.
This project did not materialise and he then considered
turning farmer and taking over one of his own farms on

his estate at Kilrush Co. Kildare. Ogilvie was becoming
a trifle importunate about Frescati. He wanted to let it
to a good tenant, and Lord Edward was annoyed
at having to show prospective occupiers over the place.
Ogilvie indeed had succeeded in interesting no less a
personage than the Lord Lieutenant himself, and Lord
Edward complained of his disappointment. In desperation he suddenly gave up his gardening, for he hated to
think that all his troubles should be for the " vile Lord
Westmoreland and the aides de camp, chaplains and all
such followers of a Lord Lieutenant. After some negotiations with his relative Conolly, the husband of his aunt
Lady Louisa, it was agreed that he should take Conolly's
lodge in Kildare town and hither Pamela and he removed
in the summer of 1794 having spent over a year in
Frescati. This was to be his permanent home until the
end.

He left Frescati with regret, but he gives an enthusiastic account of the new home in Kildare. It was a small
house, situated in the town but set well back, and it was
secluded and surrounded by some fine old elms. At the
back it was open to the country with the Curragh a short
distance off. It was a modest but very comfortable little
home in which the portrait of Tom Paine was given the
place of honour over the fireplace.

V

Lord Edward now entered on a comparatively tranquil
existence. He lived almost entirely in Kildare, he was
happy with a devoted wife and he had a little son, born
in 1794, to complete his joy. There were frequent visits
to Castletown and Carton, jaunts to Dublin, one or two
visits to England to see his mother at Malvern. There
were long walks and rides on the windy reaches of the

Curragh which stretched almost up to his doors and there were visits from beloved friends, and from other friends more aristocratic but less welcome. With the congenial friends there were gay little parties in the evenings at the Lodge, and he shocked some of his more staid aunts by associating with inferior people of the town and actually inviting them into the house. In those days there were many wandering pipers and ballad-singers going the roads in Ireland. Occasionally a piper would be invited in for the evening and Edward would send down the town for the apothecary, the butcher and his two pretty daughters and others. Then with his own sister Lady Lucy, a new friend Arthur O'Connor, to whom we shall return presently, Pamela, and the visitors, they would have what was regarded as a real Irish evening. They danced reels and hornpipes and they sang patriotic songs and old ballads. Lord Edward began at this time to take an interest in things Irish in a manner which afterwards became conventional. He always had a turf fire, and grew to like the pleasant aroma of the turf smoke. He wore green cravats and Pamela wore green ornaments. Though the link-up between the cultural heritage and the political movement was yet a long way off, he even went so far as to take an interest in the Irish language, an easy matter when one remembers that outside the towns Gaelic was spoken by ninety per cent of the population, and the small tenants on his own estate knew little English. There is no evidence that he acquired any proficiency in the language; it is noteworthy, however, that in Lord Edward's case, and even earlier in the example of Henry Flood, there are the beginnings of a Gaelic tradition.

This peaceful life might have proceeded, and Lord Edward might have continued to live the blameless exist- ence of a younger son and a country gentleman interested in gardening. He could settle into a complacent round of small visits and enjoy family gossip, The aspirations of youth would fade with middle-age, enthusiasm would give way to dullness and fine resolves be lost in petty anxieties about the health of his children. He would in short have learnt wisdom.

But the year 1794 was a turning-point not merely in the life of Lord Edward, but also in the history of his country. We have noted the Relief Act of 1793, a statute followed naturally by a period of great political activity. Not that very much had in reality been conceded, but the joy of the Catholics was so great that it blinded them to the benefits withheld. The Catholic Bishops, much to the annoyance of the United Irishmen, sent an address of profound and humble thanks, and pledged undying loyalty to His Majesty and the Constitution. The Opposition, also in a loyal mood and led by Henry Grattan, gave support to the war against France. There was indeed something like a reaction, even in Ireland, against liberal ideas and the French Revolution. The armies of France had not been doing too well in 1793. There were strange tales of the September massacres. The Bishops and middle-classes, not to speak of the gentry, opposed everything that savoured, even remotely, of French principles. But the policy of opposition to France was not altogether representative of the opinion of the peasantry. Numbers of exiled Irishmen served in the armies of France against England, and stories celebrating their exploits were recited in remote hamlets, and the country people looked to the French as their deliverers against the traditional English oppressor. Lord Edward followed the events in France with interest and he worried about the fate of his wife's father. He was pained that Orleans had voted for the death of Louis, but when Orleans's own turn came to mount the trundle-cart he was deeply troubled, not so much out of sympathy for Orleans but lest the execution might have a dangerous effect on his wife in her pregnant condition.

VI

If the years 1793-4 were calm politically there was plenty of trouble in other directions, so much so that parts of the country were drifting towards anarchy. The main cause was the activity of the Defenders, an irregular Catholic agrarian group. Despite the unifying influence of the United Irishmen, religious animosities took an ugly turn particularly in the Northern areas. The Defenders, as the name implies, were organised to resist the aggressive policy of Protestant landlords and their tenants. They were oathbound but undisciplined and they had been active on and off for a generation, succeeding other movements of a similar kind. Their activities came to overstep mere defence and in many counties they carried on a fierce agrarian war directed against rents, tithes and now against the new compulsory militia service. Their import- ance as a movement is that through this channel the Catholics eventually drifted into the militant United Irish organisation which was originally Protestant. At the beginning the United Irish movement was political. It was conceived by intellectuals who maintained that the remedy for evil lay in political agitation and national unity ; whereas Defenderism was local, even parochial, in its aims and lived by direct action. The Government saw nothing in Defenderism which was a real threat to itself, and nothing that could not be remedied by well- directed coercion and some local amelioration ; these remedies were applied and the Defender troubles began to die out in 1793 and 1794.

In the prevailing political vacuum even the United Irishmen had—so to speak—fallen on evil days, so much so that the Dublin Society feared that it would disintegrate from lack of stimulus. Besides there were the inevitable internal dissensions, and Wolfe Tone (one of the founders)

had ceased to attend the meetings, probably because of
his connection with the Catholic Committee. A short
and uneventful session of Parliament ended in March,
and the country settled down to what seemed a period of
unprecedented peace.

VII

The peaceful interlude was too good to be true and did
not last very long.

Firstly there was a noticeable increase in French
interest in Ireland. This interest had existed since the
Revolution, and off-and-on the French had sent a semi-
official emissary to review possibilities, but the reports
received had hitherto been unfavourable. Now in 1794
Ireland was visited by a certain William Jackson who
came on a mission from France. Jackson was an English
clergyman who, after a dubious career in England, had
gone to France as an ardent supporter of the Revolution
and had since lived in that country. He undertook to
go to England to spy out the land, but finding conditions
unsatisfactory, he suggested that he should go to Ireland.
Unfortunately for himself he confided in a friend named
Cockayne in London who turned informer and notified
the Government. It was decided to allow Cockayne to
accompany Jackson to Ireland, and then to permit
Jackson to operate for a spell, in the hopes that treason
would be uncovered. Jackson came, accompanied by
Cockayne, and forthwith got in touch with Wolfe Tone,
Hamilton Rowan and other United Irish leaders. Lord
Edward, it appears, refused to meet him ; then and later
he had his doubts about the efficacy of French assistance.
He thought that the Irish people ought themselves to make
the first effort. These views were prevalent in United
Irish circles, and afterwards, when French assistance was
on the way, great pains were taken to specify that the

French came as allies and not—to use the modern phrase—as ' liberators '. Indeed considerable sentiment has been wasted about this French assistance. There may have been a survival of the early revolutionary fervour to liberate all oppressed peoples, but the French general staff, quite properly, took a narrow and realistic view. There was the single question : would Ireland be a useful base from which to operate in the war against England? The Irish themselves they despised, but every delegate sent from Ireland to seek for assistance urged the importance of Ireland in the English war, both strategically and as a source of supply. They did so because the French would listen to no other argument.

Enthusiasm for the Irish adventure varied with the French general who exercised influence for the time being. Thus General Lazare Hoche was always favourable, but when Napoleon attained supreme power, interest in Ireland evaporated altogether, due chiefly at that stage to British supremacy on the sea.

Lord Edward may have had other reasons also for holding aloof from the French proposals. He may have been indignant at the execution of Orleans, particularly in view of Pamela's condition at the time. Doubtless she importuned him to be careful. By now they both knew that Lord Edward was under discreet observation and he was advised that complicity with Jackson would expose him to nothing less than a charge of treason, for the Kindgom was at war with France. That unfortunate emissary was arrested soon after arrival in Ireland, kept in prison for a year, and died in great agony from a dose of poison self-administered. He had implicated two people of importance, one was the great-souled Hamilton Rowan, a wealthy northern landlord and a genuine humanitarian, if impulsive and indiscreet. He had espoused this dangerous alliance as the only way of implementing his sense of justice for all. Actually, at the time of Jackson's arrival he was already in prison; in his too vehement support of the Parliamentary Opposition he was arrested on a charge of sedition and was now serving a two years sentence. In the curious prison routine of the period he, a rich man, lived comfortably in Newgate and Jackson even visited him there, to discuss over a bottle of wine the probabilities of a French invasion. The Castle clique nursed great resentment against Rowan, whom they regarded with the peculiar aversion reserved for the traitor to his class; for he, a wealthy Protestant aristocrat, had become the associate of papists and revolutionaries. Fitzgibbon resolved that he would make an exhibition of Rowan and have him hanged. By this intervention of Jackson there was now ample evidence against Rowan ; he was already in prison, it remained only to bring him to trial, and a trial could lead only to the gallows. In this extremity Rowan contrived a spectacular escape and made his way in a small boat to France. He was an exile for nearly twenty years and though he made his peace with the Government and was allowed to return he never altogether lost his early convictions.

The other important personage implicated was Wolfe Tone. Tone had influential friends and there may have been doubts as to the certainty of his conviction on the evidence. For whatever reason, the Government chose to deal with him leniently ; they were at this period in great uncertainty about the extent and possibilities of disaffection. Fears of the unknown are the worst fears and the authorities considered that this course was justified if they could extract from Tone a ' confession ' giving an authoritative account of the extent of a conspiracy if any. This was done, and though the confession did not disclose very much, Tone was permitted to leave the Kingdom. He did not return until he stepped down the gangway of a battered French man-o'-war in Lough Swilly on a winter day in 1798, a prisoner on his way to death.

From 1794 onwards French interest in the Irish struggle increased and this attitude had an immediate effect in Ireland. For the first time, towards the end of 1794, the United movement in Ulster began to take a definitely republican turn and to enlarge the demands for universal suffrage and reform into a complete repudiation of the connection with the English Crown. It was in this way that Irish republicanism and the modern separatist movement began. The republican theory was of very gradual emergence. When Theobald Wolfe Tone for example spoke of " breaking the connection with England " it is arguable that he was referring only to the influence of the English Cabinet on Irish affairs. He could hardly have been thinking of a constitutional connection for it was freely conceded even by Fitzgibbon, at the time of the Regency crisis, that the only binding link of the two kingdoms was that of a common monarchy, which existed also between, let us say, Britain and Hanover. There is a general fallacy in the frequent quotation of Wolfe Tone's words as applied to post-union conditions, that is to conditions entirely different from those in which they were used.

The chief advocates of republicanism were the Ulster Presbyterians, separatism had not as yet become the accepted doctrine of the Dublin Society ; as for the great mass of the Catholic population they had scarcely heard of these developments and they remained aloof and even hostile. The republican movement was enhanced when the French intimated that the help given by way of invasion was to be directed towards the setting up of an independent State and nothing less. The French made it clear that they were not interested in questions of electoral reform within the present constitution.

In these circumstances it was evident that the United Irish movement would have to be reorganised and reformed. Hitherto the objectives of the Society had been

L

limited to Parliamentary reform, the organisation was
open and the Society was not illegal. It could almost be
called a reputable Society, not unlike the Whig club. It
was now seen that a militant organisation was necessary,
pledged to bring about separatism and republicanism,
but it is important to remember that there never was
anything like unanimity on this policy ; as late as the
spring of 1798, as we shall see, overtures were made to the
Opposition in Parliament and an assurance given that if
the Constitution were reformed, militant resistance would
be called off and French help repudiated.

VIII

The second train of events which altered the course of
Irish history also began in the tranquil year 1794, and is
usually referred to by historians as the Fitzwilliam episode.
It is necessary to give a brief account of this affair.

When everything was set fair for inertia, a profound
change was brought about by a coalition of the so-called
Portland Whigs with Pitt ; the excuse given being the
better prosecution of the war. But as part of the bargain
it was agreed that the Whigs would have an opportunity
to put some of their liberal theories into practice in Ireland
and that Ireland would become as it were a Whig department. This unexpected development caused utter panic
amongst the ruling junta in Dublin, and there were vivid
recollections of the Regency debates. It was known
that the Whigs not only favoured Parliamentary reform,
which might be in any event limited, but what was
much worse they also favoured Catholic emancipation.
The Whigs themselves could argue in all fairness that
pacification and fair treatment of Ireland was essential
to the conduct of the war and the argument was unanswerable.

What followed was a melancholy tale of misunderstanding, intrigue and betrayal. The first step was the
appointment of a new Lord Lieutenant, and Lord Fitzwilliam was chosen. He was a wealthy and liberal Whig
nobleman with vast property in Ireland. He was selected
as the personal instrument to carry out the Whig policy,
he was welcomed by Grattan and his followers, by the
Catholics and indirectly by the United Irishmen ; he
may with truth be said to have received the clamourous
welcome of the Irish nation.

Ranged against Fitzwilliam in Ireland were antagonists,
few in number perhaps, but scarcely less formidable for all
that than the great multitude which welcomed him. They
were now fighting savagely in a last-ditch stand. There
was Fitzgibbon, now Lord Clare, and his battalion of
placemen and pensioners, but also there was the deep
and sinister influence of the Beresford faction. In theory
Beresford was a mere Commissioner of Revenue, (and
in this connection Dublin is indebted to him for the
Custom House designed by Gandon, for which perhaps
he may be forgiven much). But in 1794 John Beresford
was an *éminence grise* and this is a position which above
all others a man will not lightly abdicate. He had gained
power by farming the revenue, and also by stratagems like
judicious marriages, and the spreading out of offices
amongst a great network of relatives and dependents.
He had a shrewd and not unkindly personality and at least
one of his sons, John Claudius, was a friend of Wolfe Tone
and Lord Edward Fitzgerald, without of course sharing
their views. John Beresford himself was hated by the
the people with a venom which was second only to that
reserved for Lord Clare, and Clare was so accustomed to
execration that he had come to accept it as the normal
pattern of life. The surge of joy which was to arise at their
anticipated removal by Fitzwilliam was such as was never
witnessed in Ireland ; Dublin was illuminated, bonfires

blazed on the hills, men drank and women danced in the streets. Such was to be the passing of the Earl of Clare the Lord Chancellor of Ireland, and the Commissioner John Beresford.

There was a sequel. Beresford had contrived to win great personal friends in the highest circles in England, and it was said that he was in a position to intimidate even William Pitt himself. The Commissioner of Revenue had long experience of gaining his ends by quietness and thoroughness, two formidable qualities which served him well just now. Beresford was the focal point of the opposition to Fitzwilliam. It is not too much to say that the outcome of this intrigue determined the future of government in Ireland and on a wider view the whole future relationship of Ireland to England. On such minor things depends the fate of millions of people and the chances of happiness of generations unborn.

IX

It was unthinkable that any great executive officer could carry on his work if his subordinates were actively hostile, accordingly Fitzwilliam set to work without delay. He decided, perhaps prematurely, to get rid of Beresford forthwith, and to deal with Lord Clare later. Beresford was quietly removed without fuss or ostentation; he was extremely well compensated and allowed to retain the greater part of his incomings. Outwardly the Commissioner accepted his fate with philosophic resignation, he was now an old man, his sons were well provided for, what more gracious than to retire and leave the revenue to look after itself? Such were the appearances. Freed from office he strolled around Stephen's Green and greeted friends at unaccustomed forenoon hours, or browsed in bookshops : all the harmless occupations of

the recently retired. Meantime he laid his plans. He
did not waste time or thought in Dublin. Instead after
a few days he quietly took ship to England, and there he
made a round of the great Tory nobles ; the results of
this mission were soon apparent in Dublin.

Fitzwilliam in the interval had been running into
heavy weather. He had arrived in Dublin only at the end
of January 1795, and, immediately after Beresford's visit,
missives began to arrive from England indicating that
there was some misunderstanding as to his Downing
Street instructions. Fitzwilliam laid proposals before
Parliament for reform and Catholic emancipation, and
a Bill had actually received a first reading, the venal
Government majority having quickly shifted their ground.
A complicated interchange of memoranda followed with
London. These documents are available and have been
examined in the greatest detail by historical scholars and
this is not the place to go into them again. One thing is
clear, in England there was a change of heart and at the
highest level there was a fradulent claim that instructions
had been misunderstood. Pitt at first was evasive and
stammering. The decisive turn in events came when
Portland and the right-wing Whigs supported Pitt's
restraint on Fitzwilliam. The matter hastened to a swift
climax. In March Fitzwillian was peremptorily recalled
and replaced by a nonentity, Camden. The Beresford
gang was restored in all triumph, the strength of Lord
Clare was reinforced and all pretence at liberal government abandoned. The Castle prepared for coercion;
ordinary coercive measures were found inadequate and
soon the Government inaugurated a reign of terror.
Fitzwilliam left Dublin on March 20th and Dublin was a
city of mourning. That evening there were riots in the
streets. The mob sought out Clare intending to tear him
limb from limb; unable to find him they had to be content
with smashing the windows of his house and trying to

set it on fire.   All over the country wherever men were
articulate there were deep murmurings of the vengeance
to come.

The British Government has more than once acted
harshly towards Ireland and this has been excused as
due to ignorance or stupidity, but no apologist has ever
been found to explain away the Fitzwilliam affair.   It
was not a broad gesture of dominance over a subject
nation, it was merely a bit of jobbery intended to placate
a gang of placehunters.   The arrival of Fitzwilliam was
welcomed by all, Anglo-Irish and Ulster-Scot alike, by
the Protestant gentry as well as the peasants.   In the
face of this unanimity the cynicism of Pitt and the
Cabinet is breath-taking.   Judged by the test of expediency
and in the interests of Britain herself the action of the
Cabinet was nothing short of treasonable.   Britain was
embarking on a war which was soon to threaten her very
existence; invasion was imminent.   It was vital that her
western flank should be protected by a loyal nation, a
country where the enemy should seek an alliance in vain.
Ireland, Catholic as well as Protestant, was only too
willing to give such an allegiance, and her help in the
war financially, in man-power, and as a provider was in-
calculable.   Pitt was aware of all this.   It is impossible
for us to judge now by what contortions of mental pro-
cesses this politician extricated himself from the considerations.   He and his colleagues knew that they were
jeopardising the safety of the country in time of war ;   they
knew that their action would lead to a reign of terror and
civil-war in the adjacent realm.   They must have felt that
every impulse of honour and self-preservation demanded
that a tortured people be given those elementary safe-
guards which were the boast of free Englishmen.   The
action of the Cabinet in recalling Fitzwilliam led directly
to the rebellion of 1798; more remotely this recall led to
the union of Parliaments and to the century of strife and

suffering which has been the unhappy fate of two neigh-bouring islands. We may leave the subject by recalling the comment of two recent British historians who stated that Pitt " was held to have willingly persecuted those on whose side he knew justice lay and was rewarded with the peculiar hatred reserved for those who are treacherous as well as cruel."*

* Cole and Postgate: *The Common People*, p. 176. (Methuen)

X

With Fitzwilliam gone, Clare followed up the advantage by putting the Catholic menace outside the realm of practical politics. It was at this stage that he contrived to transmit the memorandum to the King in person to which we have already referred setting out that the admission of papists to Parliament would be a violation of the Coron-ation oath. With his own hand the King drafted an ungrammatical reply stating that he agreed with Fitz-gibbon's argument, and undertaking that he would never violate his conscience. This settled the fate of His Majesty's Catholic subjects in Ireland, millions of people were deprived of legislative rights at a time when the revolutionaries in France were proclaiming equailty and justice for all men.

There was now no hope of broadening the Irish Government and by the end of 1795 the struggle had become militant. On the one side there was the Irish Government, corrupt and unrepresentative, supported by placemen. Behind them were ranged all those interests which depended on Protestant ascendancy and the English connection. In the background there was the powerful support of Pitt, his British Tories and—if need be—the British army. The last sanction was the dull obstinacy of a semi-insane monarch.

This seemed a formidable combination of power, but the other side also could claim strength of a more enduring, if less obvious, sort. There were liberal-minded people, Protestant and Catholic, many of whom were restrained by the threat of disorder and fear of the unknown. There was the organised republicanism of the North, there was the immense potential of the Catholic peasantry, who, through Defenderism, were accustomed to armed activity but were restrained by the teaching of the clergy. In the background there were promises of French support and the possibility of a French landing. The United Irish who now became the spearhead of resistance were not therefore embarked on any forlorn enterprise. Indeed a fair estimate of possibilities shows that the Castle junta even with the English backing could not maintain itself, and English backing was not at all reliable. There was the fear that if the English people once came to know the purposes for which their troops were drafted to Ireland, or, if the thunderous pleas of Burke, Fox, and Sheridan (to name only three) came to be heeded, the Irish junta would be abandoned to its fate. Finally there was the moral reassurance of a just cause which would surely prevail in the end.

So, in the short space of twelve months, the political scene was radically changed; in contrast with the calm and contentment of 1794 the year 1795 closed with the threat of civil war.

fourteen

I

LIFE went on quietly at Kildare Lodge and Lord Edward spent a pleasant winter secure in the warmth of family affection. " I think " he writes " when I am down there with Pam and the child of a blustery evening with a good turf fire and a pleasant book—coming in after seeing my poultry put up, my garden settled, the place looking comfortable and taken care of I shall be as happy as possible." There are few who will quarrel with his view and few who will deny that he had hit upon the essential good things of life. At times, indeed, Pamela felt that it was too good to last though she consoled herself that there was no immediate cause for worry ; Eddy was not yet identified with any unlawful movements and there seemed little likelihood that he ever would be—the tranquil atmosphere of the Lodge was not conducive to militant revolution. To her he seemed absorbed in his home, his garden and his little son ; and he shared his great love for her with his mother only, until at times Pamela felt almost jealous. In the letter describing the pleasant winter evening he goes on to say " I regret nothing but not being near my dearest mother, and her not being of our party. It is indeed a drawback and a great one our not being more together. Dear Malvern, how pleasant we were there ;

you cannot think how this time of year puts me in mind of it.   Love always from your affectionate son."

The quiet life in Kildare continued uninterrupted despite the exciting events connected with the Fitzwilliam episode in 1795.   Lord Edward's interest in politics had waned.   He adopted the attitude of a man who is content with domestic life and to whom outside affairs are of small consequence; there are as Dr. Johnson said no such things as public worries, there are only private worries.   When rumours were current that Fitzwilliam was coming as Lord Lieutenant, he wrote to his mother to say that he was unmoved by the whole thing.   It might, he thought, make the Opposition act with more spirit and determination—a thing he had always advocated ; apart from this it would make little difference.   Wisely he did not indulge in hopes.   His opinions remained the same all through the Fitzwilliam crisis in Parliament, and when the Lord Lieutenant had departed Edward returned unperturbed to his home in Kildare, to spend a placid summer with his little family.   Yet somewhere deep within him there was conflict and dissatisfaction.   Things might thus have gone on indefinitely, but it chanced that at this time Lord Edward made a new friend who was to have a profound influence on his fate.   This friend was Arthur O'Connor.

O'Connor, the same age as Lord Edward, was a handsome and wealthy young man-about-town and a member of Parliament.   His character has been the subject of controversy, some going so far as to say that he was a traitor.   He was impulsive, individualistic and rather eccentric ;   later—in political exile—he became quarrelsome and vindictive.   But there is nothing to show that he was other than a sincere and devoted patriot.   Indeed how could it be otherwise?   He was a well-connected young man of wealth and fashion with high political talents.   His roots were deep in ascendancy privilege, and at the very outset of his career he was favoured with Government patronage. In the normal course he could look forward to a life in which elegance was suitably blended with power. All this he sacrificed; he chose to consort with papists, democrats and Paineites, and he dabbled in theories of Communism. Himself an agnostic and anti-clerical, he horrified his friends by advocating in Parliament a complete emancipation for Catholics. His ' Catholic ' speech in 1795 is deemed the turning point in his career.

With his good qualities, he was not without his foibles. One of these, to which even great minds occasionally decline, was a fetish about his descent. He concocted a theory that he was descended from a legendary pre-historic King of Ireland and such are the powers of self-persuasion that he became convinced of its truth. Accordingly he changed his name from the family name Conner, to Connor and eventually added the Irish ' O '. In point of fact his grandfather was a London chandler who made a large fortune in this useful, if uninspiring, branch of trade. It is not certain whether he was an Irishman or an Englishman but having amassed his money, he saw himself as a country gentleman and as was the practice he purchased an estate, in this case in Co. Cork.

His son, our present Arthur O'Connor's father, enhanced his social prestige and his wealth by marrying a sister of Lord Longueville. Of this marriage one son, Daniel had to flee the country on account of an affair with a neighbour's wife, another son secured a great post in the Revenue in Cork, but embezzled the funds and died in disgrace. The next son Robert was—in contrast to his brother Arthur—a violent Orangeman in Co. Cork ; he seems to have been completely unbalanced, for he spent much of his time laying informations in an effort to have his two brothers Roger and Arthur hanged. Roger who took some part in Nationalist politics, was also an eccentric and claimed to be chief of the septs of O'Connor and McCarthy More. He was the father of Fergus O'Connor the Chartist leader. There was also a sister, Anne, who being disappointed in love drowned herself in a well which is still known in Co. Cork as Anne's Well.

Against this family background it is small wonder that Arthur developed some curious ideas of his own; but endowed with his own patrimony of £1500 a year he seems to have kept clear of the family. He graduated at Trinity, and was soon identified with liberal politics. In the 1795 Parliament he definitely went over to the Opposition, and it was about this time also that he became an intimate friend of Lord Edward Fitzgerald. He delivered some left-wing speeches which not only ended his chances of political advancement, but cut him off from all personal friendships as well.

There was much in O'Connor's character and outlook which served to influence Lord Edward. As in the case of Tom Paine he was attracted by intellectual powers coupled with advanced political and social views, and being thoroughly indifferent to his own illustrious descent he could forget about O'Connor's comic fixation on the mythological Kings. A streak of eccentricity ran through the whole O'Connor family and we may be thankful that it manifested itself in this mild way in Arthur. By adopting the popular side, he was no longer welcome in the accustomed social life of Dublin and began to find his bachelor lodging lonely. He became a constant visitor to the Lodge in Kildare, and eventually went to live there altogether.

II

The session of Parliament of 1796 is noticeable for two tyrannical Acts, being the first steps taken by the Castle to inaugurate the planned reign of terror. These

statutes are known as the Indemnity Act and the Insurrection Act. Under British procedure Indemnity Acts
are always disliked and suspect. They are in the nature
of *ex post facto* legislation designed to throw the mantle
of legality over actions which when committed were
illegal. In Ireland the present Indemnity Act was intended to rectify the excesses of marauding Yeomanry
and partisan magistrates in Leinster and Connaught, and
of the Orangemen in Ulster. The Insurrection Act, it
must be admitted, contained no more than the usual
clauses in the circumstances and to law-abiding people
these provisions looked innocent enough. The sting,
however, was in the tail. The Act gave the Lord Lieutenant power to declare certain districts under martial law
and gave almost unlimited power to magistrates in such
areas to press ' suspicious characters ' into service in the
Navy. Thus the famous ' press-gangs ' appear in Irish
history; and have left such a memory that the term is still
recalled with horror. Thousands of unfortunate peasants,
chiefly from the West, were dragged away from home and
family and sent to fight England's battles on the seven
seas. The conditions in the Navy were utterly brutal, and
for a people who, though living on an island, had never
developed any love for the sea, this form of banishment
was especially cruel. The Irish fought in several naval
battles and thousands were slaughtered. They had some
slight revenge when the mutiny broke out at the Nore and
Spithead at a time of England's greatest danger—the main
force among the lower ranks of mutineers was the Irish.

Lord Edward spoke in the debate on the second of these
Acts, a moderate speech when one recalls earlier utterances and more restrained than the speeches of some
others in Opposition. Opposing the Bill he said that
" nothing would tranquilize the country but the sincere
endeavour of the Government to redress the grievances
of the people. If that was done, the people would return

to their allegiance ;—if not he feared that neither Resolutions nor Bills would be of any avail."

These two measures finally determined O'Connor and Lord Edward. They joined the United Irishmen, or to put it more accurately, they became formally identified with that body. They were not initiated in the usual way, for the United Society was now an oath-bound body and in their case the oath, it seems, was dispensed with ; O'Connor stated later that he never took an oath and that Lord Edward was also exempted. It is certain however, that they were very soon deeply involved in the work of the United Irishmen. A Leinster directory was formed and both were made members and it was agreed that Lord Edward would not only lend the prestige of his name, but also provide that military experience which was urgently required. Lord Edward's talents, then, as always, were especially military.

The United Irish movement was gaining in strength but the Defenders were not yet officially incorporated. This was a source of worry to leaders who had set out to unite all true men against tyranny and who wished to stave off the excuse for martial law and terrorism brought on by agrarian outbreaks. Defenderism was unorganised, scattered and spontaneous ; it was effective within certain limits but it suffered from the heavy condemnation of the Church authorities. The Sacraments were refused and men were even left to go to the scaffold without the consolations of religion. There had been, to illustrate, an outstanding case the previous year in Lord Edward's own neighbourhood. Lawrence O'Connor was a poor schoolmaster at Naas, one of those obscure visionaries who turn up so often in the history of the period, fighting against overwhelming odds and in the end sacrificing their lives. Lawrence O'Connor's chief concern was the condition of the peasantry and the tyranny of the rack-renters and landlords. Political matters, even the question of reform or emancipation of Catholics were a secondary consideration. He was charged with administering an illegal oath, tried at Naas in 1795, and duly sentenced to be hanged. He made a remarkable speech from the dock, pointing to the sincerity of his motives, and detailing the wrongs of the poor people which sooner or later must be removed. The speech had a startling effect even on his prosecutors, and Judge Finucane, who tried the case, was moved to tears. Even though penitent, O'Connor had to go to the gallows without the Sacraments, as no Catholic priest would minister to him.

Strenuous efforts were now made to incorporate the Defenders in the United Irish. The celebrated James Napper Tandy was a pioneer in this activity, going so far, it is said, as himself to take a Defender oath, The Government got to hear of it, and, since Tandy was also involved in the Jackson affair, he had to flee the realm. Coinciding with this reorganisation the Castle was also busy. A Government which feels insecure when faced with a conspiracy generally seeks to establish a sort of private army made up of its own supporters. Where grievances are social and political the regular army may not always be reliable. These armed forces reappear in history in various guises, and their common characteristic is brutality. In the Ireland of the late seventeen-nineties the force known as the Yeomanry has earned a high place in the annals of barbarism. Theoretically, the Yeomanry was open to all loyal citizens; in fact it was made up almost exclusively of Orangemen and Castle supporters. Nevertheless it soon became a formidable and relatively efficient body, better suited to the kind of work which it was called on to perform than regular troops, and certainly more suitable than troops drafted from England. The English troops, from a Government point of view, suffered from too great a discipline and to make matters worse they were occasionally commanded by humane

Generals like Sir John Moore or General Abercromby
who, horrified by what they witnessed protested strongly
to the Castle.

After the Jackson affair, the United Irish Society,
though not formally suppressed, was made virtually
illegal ; but even earlier the Government agents were on
the track, and we note that in May 1794 a meeting in
Taylor's Hall in Dublin was, with doubtful legality,
broken up by the police. The Fitzwilliam episode may
be said to have ended the constitutional phase. The
United Irish Society became militant, but it is important
to note that this military impetus came from the North.
The Society was better organised in Ulster and the Ulstermen were impatient. They suffered from none of the
inhibitions—such as loyalty to a lawful monarch—
which to the end afflicted the Catholic masses in the South.
Looking at it now it is evident that the United Irish
Society never took any hold in the South or West, or even
a real hold in Leinster. But despite the Republican urge
in the North, the leaders generally were for long reluctant
to be committed to a method of physical force and the
United Irishmen clung almost desperately to hopes of
constitutional change. The people wished simply to
live as contented subjects of His Majesty. This sub-
missive attitude did not however fall in with the plans of
those in power in the Castle and the charge is freely made
that the excesses of the Yeomanry and the technique of
the reign of terror were used to goad the people into
premature rebellion, and it is asserted that William Pitt
and the British Cabinet were privy to this counter conspiracy. A premature rebellion, a prostrate people and
the annihilation of the United Irishmen were tempting
objectives, for not only would the existing regime be
preserved for at least a generation, but the union of
parliaments and the destruction of the Irish nation as a
separate entity would follow.

After 1796, and despite this hesitancy in the Dublin Society, the civil organisation of the United Irishmen ceased. Henceforward the units were military both in their structure and objective. The organisation was carefully and cleverly designed to ensure loyalty and trust and—if possible—secrecy, but these efforts to preserve mystery absorbed a considerable part of the strength of the movement. The Government knew almost everything and one queries whether the credulity of the United leaders was so great as to believe that the Government knew little. Yet it is surprising that the Castle, knowing so much, seemed at the crisis unaware of the essentials. The authorities tended to exaggerate the extent and gravity of the conspiracy (it often suits a government to pretend that the danger is much greater than in fact it is) while at the same time they seemed unaware of the real menace.

For this, the Government could thank the great army of informers. It was the very flowering time of this species ; never was the range of informers so wide, never were their activities so prolonged. The public, that is to say, the poor, were taxed heavily to provide the revenues which then and subsequently were given away in rewards and pensions. The informers came from all ranks. They included patriot leaders standing high in the ranks of the United men, like Leonard McNally and Reynolds, and there were humble day-labourers and tramping-men. There were informers in the aristocracy and clergy. There were Englishmen and Scots. The racket was the heaven-sent refuge for bankrupt merchants, discredited journalists and lawyers, and strange characters who revenged themselves for disappointment and obscurity, and with their gains endeavoured to set up as gentlemen and squires. There was no blood-money which the informer would refuse, and the record is sometimes horrifying. Reynolds, a connection of Lord Edward betrayed the Leinster Directory and went

M

into the box and sent three of them to the gallows; Magan betrayed Lord Edward; and, perhaps worse than either, Leonard McNally under the seal of confidence betrayed Robert Emmet, and then pretended to defend him at his trial.

III

When O'Connor and Lord Edward joined with the United Irishmen the organisation had become military. Other able men joined about the same time, notably Thomas Addis Emmet and Dr. McNevin. Inevitably opinion began to divide within the inner circles; there were those who wanted an appeal to arms at once, and there was a conservative element indulging yet further hopes of constitutional change. Arthur O'Connor and Lord Edward were foremost in the activist party, and the chief advocate of the conservative view was the ablest leader of the United Irishmen, and indeed one of the greatest men of his generation, Thomas Addis Emmet. Perhaps the most melancholy reflection on this period is that the talents and sincere purposes of this man should perforce be given over to this dangerous and wasteful type of conspiracy, and to activities for which he was really unsuited. Abilities which would have been at the service of his fellows were frittered away in dangers, in long imprisonment and in the dreariness of exile. It is some consolation to reflect that even these misfortunes did not end his career, and that afterwards he rose to be Attorney General of New York State.

Divided as they were on the question of recourse to arms, there was one subject on which there was now something like unanimity. This was assistance by the French. The early French enthusiasm to help oppressed nations had abated ; the feeling, probably sincere at the time, had through a welter of anarchy and massacre

grown into a lust for foreign conquest. Still when combined with a mortal blow at England the sacred mission
to assist the downtrodden proved irresistible. France was
now, and would be for many years to come, a dangerous
enemy on land. Her armies on the Continent were everywhere triumphant, and the coalition against her had
broken up. Belgium was annexed, the Emperor was
silenced, the independence of Holland was taken away,
and Bonaparte had his first victories in Italy. France
was in possession of the coast from the Texel to the
Pyrenees. Britain had the consolation, unimportant as
it seemed at the time, of triumph in the far-flung colonies,
her adventurous squadrons seized not only the French
settlements but most of the Dutch colonies as well ;
what was more, England held on to them when the long
drawn-out struggle ended in the Congress of Vienna. From
this era dates the importance of the British Empire overseas.

Meantime Britain seemed in dire peril, with little hope
of recovery. She dare not show troops on the Continent,
and, though triumphant on the seas, her fleets were badly
organised and mutinous. Pitt therefore was desperately
anxious for a peace; he needed a respite to preserve the
integrity of the homeland, and, maybe, the new-found
Empire ; yet every month brought news of further
French triumphs. Britain in the end was obliged to
sue for peace and to suffer the humiliation of having her
overtures scornfully rejected.

French interest in Ireland was intermittent, but it never
entirely faded. As far back as 1793, French investigations
of the Irish possibility had begun when Oswald, an
American, was sent over from France ; his report was
not favourable and enthusiasm flagged. It was revived
again by the news of the United Irish movement,
but the task of persuading the French proved none too
easy until the tempo was increased by the eloquent
pleadings of Wolfe Tone.

After Oswald, the next emissary of importance was William Jackson, to whose case we have already referred. Jackson's visit had at least one result—it scattered to the Continent three men who were destined to raise French interest in Ireland to the highest point. These men were Wolfe Tone, James Napper Tandy, and to a lesser extent, Hamilton Rowan. Of Rowan it may be said that, after his narrow escape from the gallows, he modified his interest in Irish politics. Tone had been banished to America but he very soon tired of the life of a small-time farmer, and the United Irish leaders heard with enthusiasm that Tone was now conducting vigorous negotiations with the French agents in Philadelphia, but to what extent he had succeeded was uncertain. In the beginning of 1796 Tone left America to push his representations at the centre of activity in Paris. The prospects of assistance could not be known in Ireland, and it was decided therefore that two prominent leaders of the United men, preferably men of individual prestige and position should get in touch with the French. The two selected were Arthur O'Connor and Lord Edward Fitzgerald. The whole scheme was suggested by Arthur O'Connor, for he was an impetuous young man and was annoyed at what he thought was the procrastination of the United leaders, and their reluctance to use force. This attitude could always be defended by the conservatives by reference to the imminence of French aid. O'Connor sought to test the sincerity of French assurances and at the same time determine this important matter finally.

fifteen

I

IN or about the month of May 1796 Lord Edward and Arthur O'Connor set out on their mission to make contact with the French. The rendezvous was Hamburg. Lord Edward went first to London accompanied by Pamela, then far advanced in her second pregnancy; but O'Connor travelled separately. The object in taking Pamela on this hazardous expedition was to lend colour to the excuse that the Hamburg journey was really a visit to his mother-in-law Madame de Genlis. This lady was then living there, arranging for the forthcoming marriage of her daughter to a wealthy burgess, and in her memoirs she affects to be much pleased and touched by the filial duty of Pamela in making this journey.

For Lord Edward and O'Connor this was a dangerous and definitely treasonable expedition, and it brought them within the ambit of the criminal law. The punishment for treason was death. The authorities in both Dublin and London were watching them closely, being of course in possession of the plans before ever the two delegates left Ireland. The Government naturally enough took a serious view of the business. Dabbling with subversive politics in Dublin was one thing, treating with the King's enemies in time of war, particularly a war that was going

disastrously, was clearly another matter. Lord Edward
they might regard as a hot-headed, even a well-meaning,
young man, married to a doubtful French wife—a young
man who conceivably might out-grow this phase of
radicalism. Besides he had powerful connections, ex-
tending up to royalty itself, he had given good service in
the army and he had a genuine grievance. However,
negotiating with the French enemy was going a bit far,
and was more than a Government would overlook.
The Castle therefore took counsel of Downing Street and
Pitt as usual was for holding back. Pitt was aware that the
city of Hamburg, with the whole French coast and even
Paris itself, was packed with British agents of one kind or
another, and that no great harm could be done by leaving
the travellers have their head and uncovering the possibilities of French aid.

Of O'Connor the Castle party took a more stern view,
and it is possible that even at this early stage of his supposed treason they were eager to have him arrested.
O'Connor may have been unaware of this, but his turn
was to come a year later when he had a narrow escape
from the gallows. At the moment, the Government
recognised in O'Connor a more dangerous type than
Lord Edward, for he was undoubtedly a man of ability
and determined purpose. What strikes one forcibly at
this stage is how both the leaders could have been so
ingenuous as to believe, or at least to act as if they believed,
that the Government knew little or nothing. Particularly is
this surprising in the case of O'Connor who must have known
in Dublin that he was being watched. Espionage leads to
counter espionage and the United men had their informers
too ; but the naïveté of many of the Irish leaders is
one of the most puzzling features of this whole epoch.

Lord Edward and his wife stayed *en route* in London
for a short time. His friends were worried at his air of
preoccupation, and it seems that it was common knowledge

that he was now engaged on this mission. One evening he dined with his cousin Charles James Fox, Richard Brinsley Sheridan also being present ; afterwards he confided in Fox. This may be excused as Fox at this period was himself on the brink of treasonable activities, but one fears that Lord Edward may have been sufficiently foolish to confide in the good-natured but irresponsible Sheridan. He also, of course, visited Devonshire House. There Pamela, attractive as ever, but obliged to take things easy, was taken aside for a little serious chat by no less a person that His Royal Highness the Duke of York. The Duke told her frankly that they all knew about the mission of dear Eddy. They sympathised with his efforts to overthrow the corrupt junta in Dublin, but he entreated her to try and dissuade Eddy at least from going so far as to enter French territory. By doing so, the Prince explained, he would be putting himself at the mercy of the Castle, and lay himself open to a charge of high treason. What Pamela replied to this startling disclosure is not recorded. Then, as afterwards, there is silence about her whole attitude in those dangerous times, but there is no doubt that she was privy to the negotiations at Hamburg. One must presume that she did not entirely disapprove. A pregnant girl, wife of a devoted husband, might easily have persuaded him not to embark on the mission, or at least she herself would have been justified in staying at home. Madame de Genlis records that Pamela adopted a dual attitude of ignorance and non-interference in Eddy's affairs; ignorance lest she should be of use to the authorities if they questioned her, and non-interference on the principle of wifely self-effacement, and also in deference to a certain streak of stubbornness in Eddy's nature where matters touching the United movement were concerned. Madame approves of Pamela's attitude which, thus neatly put, had the appearance of being her own invention. It seems scarcely credible that in her condition Pamela would not have preferred a quiet life in the domesticity of Kildare, yet as she did in fact accompany her husband to Hamburg, one must conclude that she shared, however tacitly, his enthusiasm for an Irish Revolution.

Arthur O'Connor also sojourned in London *en route*, and he also conferred with the Whig leaders. In London he made a new and important acquaintance. He went to dinner at the Duchess of Leinster's house in Harley Street, and amongst the members of the family present to receive him was Lord Edward's younger and, with Sophia, favourite sister, Lady Lucy Fitzgerald, then an attractive young lady aged twenty-five, with masses of beautiful brown hair. She was impressionable, rather sentimental, and, more than any member of the family, she shared Lord Edward's advanced views. At the moment she was recovering from an unfortunate love-affair with a certain faithless Mr. Wodehouse, and it is a measure of her trust that she still recorded optimistically in her diary that it was Mr. Wodehouse's *soul* that was so attractive in him. Her description of Arthur, taken as a first impression, is not illuminating. She records simply that " he was a great friend of Eddy's " and, of course, a " great democrat " and also that he was the man " who made the famous speech " (this refers to O'Connor's pro-Catholic speech in 1795.) The ' great democrat ' however, made a deeper impression on Lucy than was evident at the time; he had much to recommend him to any romantic young lady. He was young and handsome, he spoke portentously about grave matters which were only half-understood by Lucy: he liked an audience and she supplied it. She possessed that surest attraction for men: a gift of reasonably intelligent conversation, and she had the art of listening and making a man's preoccupations seem important even though secretly she thinks them ridiculous. She knew that he and Eddy were setting out on the mission to France; she was in the mood for flirtation, and she resolved to waylay them on the return journey, and to see more of Arthur.

II

In Hamburg Lord Edward made immediate contact with Reinhardt, the French Minister to the Hanseatic Towns. O'Connor, it should be mentioned, had not yet arrived ; he travelled independently from London and he preserved considerable secrecy about his journey. Lord Edward meantime had given an optimistic account of the Irish scene to Reinhardt, but that gentleman was none too favourably impressed. Still he deemed the matter of sufficient importance to prepare an elaborate memorandum for the French Foreign Office. That department was now at length treating the Irish case very seriously. A copy of this useful memorandum promptly reached the hands of Mr. Pitt, how we do not know, but in such circumstances as to render Reinhardt himself open to the charge of treachery. This accusation has never been proved, and it now appears that he was merely guilty of carelessness of a kind amounting to crime. This document is remarkable also for some side-lights on the character of Lord Edward. Reinhardt had formed a very favourable impression of Lord Edward as a man, and his personal view has often been quoted. It should be remembered that Reinhardt was a sophistic-ated diplomat and that he had served in a hard revolution-ary school where adolescence is a brief or even a non-existent interlude. He describes Lord Edward as a young man incapable of perfidy and for whose loyalty he would answer with his head. At the same time it appeared to him that Lord Edward was devoid of any

qualities of leadership, or special talents, and was unfit
to be in charge of a great enterprise.

A month later Arthur O'Connor appeared on the
scene, and in contrast with Lord Edward, O'Connor
struck Reinhardt as being a man of great ability, This
caused Reinhardt to modify his opinion as to the importance of the mission. He addressed a further dispatch to
De La Croix, the French Foreign Minister, giving a
favourable report of the Irish situation, but he noted that
O'Connor stressed that the French were coming only as
allies to help a people who could liberate themselves.
For some reason O'Connor was extremely anxious to get
to Paris. Perhaps he believed that after so much inde-
cision no really conclusive undertaking could be obtained
from intermediaries; but he must have realised that to go
to Paris in the circumstances would have amounted to
political exile. In the end the occasion did not arise. What
O'Connor apparently did not know was that independently
of the two delegates in Hamburg Wolfe Tone had been
pushing his case feverishly in Paris, and the Directory had
already decided on an Irish expedition. Naturally Tone
was questioned about the two emissaries who had suddenly
appeared in Hamburg. At first he was rather taken
aback that negotiations, of which he had not heard, had
been in progress ; but when asked if the delegates were
trustworthy he gave the highest praise to each. He seems
to have been only slightly acquainted with them—a fact
which has caused comment but which is not surprising
when one remembers that Tone had to leave Ireland
after the arrest of Jackson in 1794, a considerable
time before the United movement had become
revolutionary.

O'Connor meantime was once more insisting either
on a visit to Paris or else that arrangements should be
made for him to meet one of the Directory or a General
in some convenient rendezvous. But by now a slight if

unexpected difficulty presented itself to the French authorities. From the beginning the French seem to have been
uneasy, if not exactly suspicious, about Lord Edward.
This arose from his rank and connections. Moreover the
French leaders had vivid and unpleasant memories of the
activities of their own noble *émigrés* abroad. A fresh
cause of uneasiness now appeared: Lord Edward was
married to a daughter of Egalité and the Directory
feared that in any negotiations with him they might seem
to be involving themselves in Orleanist plots. These
doubts were so far-fetched that soon all difficulties were
smoothed over, and the two delegates set out from
Hamburg for Switzerland where it was agreed that
negotiations would recommence personally with some
higher authorities. In Basle they met Barthélemy, then
French Minister in Switzerland, and arrangements were
made that O'Connor should meet no less a person than
General Hoche himself on the French frontier. Hoche
was at first reluctant to meet Lord Edward, but this was
also arranged, and O'Connor thereupon abandoned his
plan of going to Paris. The net result of the meeting
with Hoche was a definite undertaking that the French
would forthwith dispatch an expedition in great strength
to Ireland—Hoche having always been favourable to the
idea. The two Irishmen, much gratified, turned their
steps towards home.

They made a short tour through Switzerland and then
parted for the moment, Lord Edward travelled alone on
the return journey in leisurely stages along the pleasant
valley of the Rhine, then at the height of summer glory.
Not quite alone, however. In his coach there was
another passenger, a pleasant mature woman, shy and
rather reserved in manner and not, it seemed, disposed
to general conversation. Fitzgerald, the unique conspir-
ator, was, as always, anxious to be helpful and kindly ;
his successful mission and the prospect of reunion with

his wife and a visit to his mother in London had given him an elevation of spirit. In this mood he was prone to talk, but his fair companion seemed bored with his hints at great happenings and the purposes of his journey. There was much small talk about the beauty of the Rhineland scenery. Only rarely out of idle curiosity and in between yawns, as it were, she would put him a half-formed question, and the gay revolutionary unthinking would reply. He was completely at ease; if he mentioned Ireland she seemed confused and wished he would change the subject and get on to more pleasant things. Still her interest increased at times and she put him quite a few questions on the relationship of Ireland with France. He thoroughly enjoyed the trip.

When he arrived in Hamburg, however, he quickly changed his tune. The astute Madame de Genlis had a serious conversation with him about the trip from Basle. She was versed in the wiles of political conspiracy, and amongst other things she quickly elicited that he had met a charming young matron on the journey who seemed to enjoy occasional discussion on the countryside and the general chat of travellers, but who grew bored and reserved whenever he hinted at more serious topics. The experienced Madame recognised the technique ; she felt all that annoyance which one feels when confronted with well-meaning stupidity. One or two questions to her son-in-law gave her all that she wanted to know. She realised that the affair had a very serious side, and she was truly alarmed. Her annoyance increased when she found that even then Eddy would not be convinced, but the clever Madame knew that there was little now to be gained by recriminations, and that no man likes to be proved a fool. She left the matter at that, trusting that the incident might serve as a caution.

The fellow-traveller was of course a British agent ; a discarded mistress of one of William Pitt's Cabinet colleagues, who had received this special assignment. Pitt was evidently leaving nothing to chance, but we do not know how much Lord Edward divulged. What we do know is that while O'Connor and Fitzgerald were getting ready to come home, pleased with the success of their secret mission, the authorities in Dublin Castle and London were scrutinising detailed reports of their activities abroad and the plans for the proposed invasion.

sixteen

I

LORD Edward returned to Hamburg and escaping from Madame de Genlis he found to his great joy that he was a father once again. During his absence Pamela had given birth to her second child, a daughter, also named Pamela. Lord Edward wrote off enthusiastic letters to his mother telling her that his sweet Pam was overjoyed to see him, and giving her his own account of the Swiss visit. O'Connor had stayed behind in Switzerland, making as Lord Edward put it, another tour. " There never were two persons ", he wrote " who more thouroghly enjoyed Switzerland than we did. We saw it with true Rousseau enthusiasm : he is as fond of Rousseau as I am so you may conceive how we enjoyed the journey." Lord Edward, Pamela and the newly-arrived daughter left Hamburg in August and stayed a short time in Harley Street and at Malvern with his mother, leaving for Ireland in September. By arrange-ment they left the first-born son, Eddy, in care of his grandmother the Duchess, who, perhaps because she had given birth to twenty-one children herself, seemed happiest when she had an infant about the place. About a month later Arthur O'Connor arrived back in Ireland from his travels, so, after the exciting negotiations abroad, and with the portent of great deeds ahead, the friends were together again. It was autumn on the Kildare plains, and Lord Edward looked forward to a homely winter, varied this time with his United Irish activities. At the same time he reflected that the French were preparing to invade, and that at any moment he might go out from this quiet retreat in no less a capacity than commander-in-chief of the insurgent forces of Ireland.

Arthur O'Connor was now spending most of his time at the Lodge, and the party had received another important addition. Lady Lucy, to be sure, had met Arthur again passing through London, and about a fortnight later she too crossed to Ireland. The excuse given was her promise to pay a prolonged visit to her aunt in Castletown, Celbridge—where in fact she stayed for a time—but her real reason, it is needless to say, was to be near Arthur. After a short stay in Celbridge she too removed to the Lodge and the party was complete. Lucy calls it the " beloved quoituor " (*sic*). She was in love again and Mr. Wodehouse was quite forgotten.

Inevitably there was gossip ; some of Lord Edward's aunts grew alarmed and began to write gentle little warning letters to Lucy; curiously enough they were not fearful for Lucy's virtue, but they trembled for the influence that the horrid Mr. O'Connor—a notorious democrat—might have on her mind. Lord Edward of course they considered as past saving. As for Pamela she was French and that explained everything. Poor Lucy was bewildered and scared, rather than attracted, by all this ' democracy '. She never really understood how men could get so worked up over political problems; she regarded politics as remote from the essence of life, which in her case meant personal relationships and family gossip. She shared O'Connor's enthusiasms, and she loved and admired Eddy, and consequently would embrace any cause in which they were interested. She was a shrewd little observer herself, and like many such women she perceived in O'Connor the qualities of leadership and intellect ; these things instinctively attracted her even though she reflected with a sigh that they conflicted with hopes of marriage and a quiet life. She had to contend with the age-old problems of a woman in love with a man of action.

Moreover she was frequently worried. She was not particularly religious, but she had no inclination to question the dogmatic tenets she had been taught. They did not matter a great deal or interfere with one's life, therefore why throw them overboard and find oneself in a strange outer darkness? She was troubled by Arthur's vehement agnosticism which she could not understand, but she regarded it chiefly as irreligion. Actually O'Connor argued that worldly questions should be kept on a worldly plane, and that one cannot, in defence of social innovation, give battle to an antagonist who calls in the aid of Heaven. So much seemed reasonable, yet the Almighty for some reason was always averse to social change, that is to say He desired that the rich should continue to be rich and the poor continue to be poor. O'Connor's grievance was an ancient one, namely that Churches had called down heavenly sanctions on a superstitious people to perpetuate evil in this world. Lucy was perplexed and then melancholy. Arthur still was her hero and she reflected that it was a sad thing to see such a great mind given over to doctrines like these.

What O'Connor thought of her is not apparent and there is little evidence that he thought of her seriously at all. At the moment his mind was intent on an armed rising. He was one of the left-wing active party of the United leaders; he desired French aid, but, with it or without it, he was satisfied there would be no change without recourse to arms. None of the United men denied this, the question was " When? ", and this, as we shall see, developed into a bitter struggle. While his thoughts were elsewhere on acts of danger and possible glory, he could not delay with an amiable little body like Lady Lucy—the aunts could therefore set their minds at rest. O'Connor was not at the moment thinking of marriage, and being temperate he did not indulge outside marriage. Lucy may have guessed and pondered and occasionally have been a little disappointed, but she does not seem to have worried much.

II

On the surface, existence at the Lodge was uneventful. Lady Lucy first stayed some time at Castletown, the great house of the Conollys, five miles or so from Carton, and then went to stay at Carton. She became curious and a little frightened at the alarming and mysterious political situation and she feared most of all for Eddy. Her journal gives a picture of their private lives :—

" Castletown Oct. 23—I feel so happy to be at dear Castletown. It so reminds me of the Days of my Child-hood. The Edwards came, and the Castlereaghs and Papa. He and I made it up. Aunt Louisa and I went to Carton in the morning.

" Oct. 29—Edward and I walked to Carton, and saw Lord Clare. We had an amusing snug chat as we went our way.

" Carton, Nov. 20—We were a delightful party. Ly. Edward was there the whole time and Ed. backwards and forwards : we had beautiful dancing and such a Ballet call'd Didone. Ly. Ed. composed it mostly, I selected the music.

" Nov. 21—I went to town. Mr. Ogilvie gave us a snack at Leinster House. Ly. Ed. came to town too. Mr. O'Connor came to see her, but we did not see *him*, as Mr. Ogilvie would not invite him in.

" Nov. 27—Ly. Ed. and I left Carton and came to Kildare where we found Mr. O'Connor and Edward."

Behind these unaffected entries there is a suggestion of uneasiness, and resentment amongst Lord Edward's connections. His brother Leinster was a quiet and unassuming man. Though he had long since parted company with the Government faction he strongly disapproved of Eddy's activities and carried his disapproval so far that he and his brother were not even on speaking terms. Ogilvie was even more forthright. He was now a man of consequence but he had a venomous hatred for Dublin and everything Irish; not a political bias, but because the place and the people recalled his early days of dependence. Above all he had no patience with revolutionaries.

The other person mentioned by Lucy was a comparative newcomer, Robert Stewart, Viscount Castlereagh, the heir to the Marquis of Londonderry. Castlereagh was the same age as Lord Edward. He entered Parliament at the age of twenty-one, and commenced his career on the popular side. He soon mended his hand. Now he was a grave young man, married to a daughter of a former Chief Secretary, and was himself soon to be Acting Chief Secretary. He had industry and application, a certain political acumen, and ruthlessness ; he had a handsome appearance and great wealth, but more important than any of these advantages he had a knack of cultivating personal friendships in the right places, and he early became a confidant of Lord Clare and William Pitt. His political future was accordingly assured if only these friends would retain power. Political opportunity in Ireland was limited but in that country Robert Stewart has left an undying name as the chief executive of Pitt's scheme to bring about the Union. In politics no deception was too shameful, no breach of faith too horrible for this young man. He never winced at the extent of the bribery or questioned the money paid out of the public funds to informers and political hacks in defiance of all decency. He had an objective in view, he had been told that it must be attained ; as to the means, they did not matter. The consequences did not matter either— these are measured as a century or more of pillage and suffering for an entire people. The Union accomplished, Robert Stewart Viscount Castlereagh passed from the local arena, moving on to greater fame as British Foreign Secretary. To the Irish this latter phase is of no consequence—he is remembered only for his exploits at home.

Lord Castlereagh, like many others, had a sincere liking for Lord Edward; and Lady Castlereagh, his young and beautiful wife, had, contrary to the general feeling in Dublin an even greater affection for Pamela. The Castlereaghs visited at Castletown and Carton, they even visited the ' beloved quoituor ' at Kildare. We can imagine the scene, the gay familiarity and small talk of the women, the kindly bewilderment of Lady Lucy and the suave graciousness of Castlereagh himself. The conversation usually kept clear of current politics. Even in the unthinkable event of Arthur and Lord Edward suddenly turning informers they could not tell Castlereagh much that he did not know ; he could study all their secrets, including the recent negotiations with the French, by driving back to the Castle and calling for the private dispatches. But in the autumn quietness of the Kildare room, broken only by the winds blowing from the spacious acres of the Curragh, the conversation waxed gay and merry. At times Castlereagh's mind would stray back to the dossiers and between smiles he would estimate if there was sufficient evidence, as things stood, to send both his hosts to the gallows. Treason even then was a difficult offence to prove home. The trial would be by jury and corroborative evidence would be required—

in England two witnesses, in Ireland one. Castlereagh reflected on the vexatious difficulty they were having in the Castle in getting people to go into the witness-box.

Lady Castlereagh, her interests being otherwise, noted the glances that passed between Lucy and Arthur and in the carriage on the way home—despite the seeming lack of interest on her husband's part—she was unable to converse about anything else. Castlereagh was anxious. In one man he recognised his intellectual superior ; in the other he saw one whose popularity was linked to ancient and romantic lineage. If, according to the laws of the realm, there was evidence enough to hang them or even to keep them in prison then why not strike *now*? This indeed was a question frequently discussed in conclave at the Castle. To dispose of the leaders here and now would put an end to the incipient revolt and make a French conquest more difficult. But there were other considerations and the stakes were high. Whenever drastic action was proposed the English Government always said " Wait ". Besides, although there would be no mercy for O'Connor, few of the junta really wished to see Lord Edward hanged. Lord Clare himself—a man not especially noted for tenderness of spirit—went so far as to travel specially to Castletown and Carton and plead with the frightened aunts. The matter, in Clare's view, was a simple one ; Lord Edward even now had only to leave the country and the ports were open.

From a Government point of view there was great wisdom in this advice, for the defection of Lord Edward at this stage would have been an irreparable blow to the United Irish movement. To the end Clare possessed a certain regard for Lord Edward, professing to treat him as a well-meaning, if misguided youth. Clare was a man who had little patience with half-measures. He perceived in Fitzgerald a hardihood, nobler in quality, but akin to his own.

III

If then, during that winter of '96, the surface of Lord Edward's life seemed to be uneventful, there was much going on underneath. He and O'Connor lived in a state of great mental excitement, but their activities, as we say nowadays were underground. There was an immense task before them. There is some indication of how life proceeded in Lady Lucy's journal, but there was much that she did not dare to record. Strange men would arrive stealthily at the Lodge—sometimes at midnight—men of military bearing and stern demeanour, and oftentimes with hard northern accents. They would be closeted with Lord Edward and O'Connor for hours together in the room below. The two women in bed upstairs would be unable to sleep from anxiety, and the muffled sounds of conversation would occasionally be heard. Lucy would breathe a prayer that God might protect dear Eddy and Arthur. Eventually the men would depart into the night and Eddy and O'Connor would stumble up to bed. Sometimes Eddy would be away for days on end. Lucy's spirit would droop, and Pamela as she tended the infant daughter was pale with worry. In a day or two he would return, tired but elated. Sometimes Arthur went to Dublin and was absent for a week or more. The women did not, as a rule, put questions to Eddy. There was a deep understanding as to the limits within which curiosity would be justified; even the claims of wifely love and sisterly devotion did not excuse questioning. There were many subjects which were not mentioned at all, and we may doubt if at this period his wife and friends could realise how deeply he was involved.

The name of the Geraldine was legend, and in the North that name was passed on from circle to circle in the United Irishmen as that of the leader who had received

his military training with the British, had served gallantly
in the field, and was now to be commander-in-chief of
the insurgent army.   In the South, except in Dublin the
Society was not so numerous nor so well organised.
But Lord Edward's influence was everywhere, his name
was whispered, secretly perhaps. but it was known.   In
the East and South too the folklore was rich in memories
of the great days of the Fitzgeralds, and there were old
prophecies that a Geraldine would one day arise to
set Ireland free.   An affection, a deep personal loyalty,
developed for Lord Edward amongst the common people,
particularly the peasantry, and it is still alive today.
Even he, who was utterly devoid of any self-esteem or
vanity could not but notice the reverent glances he received
from the day-labourers and drovers when he took his
exercise canter on the Curragh, or the loyal salutes he
received when he walked the streets of the town of
Kildare ;   or when, accompanied by Lucy or Pamela,
he took a winter stroll along the country roads.

There was however little time for strolling.   The
French were expected hourly, and the rising must take
place.   The insurgent army had to be mobilised and
prepared and arms distributed.   It became clear
to Lord Edward, now that the French invasion was
imminent, that there could be no rising until the French
arrived, but if the French came in force as they intended,
there would be little use for the irregular Irish auxiliaries.
If the French landed it was reasonably certain that they
would overrun the country.

This fateful winter of 1796 wore on, the days grew
shorter, the nights more stormy.   On Nov. 27, as we
have seen, Lucy recorded that she and Pamela left Carton
and came to Kildare, where they found Arthur and Eddy.
Nothing, she says, could be more comfortable than the
little habitation, and when evening came Arthur O'Connor

read to them Shakespeare's *Julius Cæsar*. The next day they took a walk on the Curragh—a walk of ten miles to see Mr. Daly's lodge—and in the evening they had a piper in and they all danced jigs. The following day they were out again, this time riding. Edward and Lucy kept together and Pamela and Arthur (so Lucy says), and they kept talking for hours mostly about Hamburg and the people they met there. The following night was a sort of gala night—" we had " says Lucy, " quite a ball ; we made up 7 couple calling in servants and maids." The Christmas season drew near. Their time alternated between walking and riding, reading and argument, with mild junketings in the evening ; altogether, one would think a pleasant enough existence.

In December Arthur and Edward departed suddenly on what Lucy calls a Tour and were absent for over a week. The business of the " tour " turned out to be an inspection of some of the United Irish Societies and the usual routine of organization. Their trip extended to Connaught where the Society was so weak as to be, for all practical purposes, non-existent; and amongst other things they called on a gentleman whom Lucy describes as the " King of Connaught ". This man's name was O'Connor, and Arthur took him and his pretences seriously, and was duly impressed—Lord Edward, disciple of Paine, presumably taking a different view. The King preserved due gravity, greeting them formally with " Arthur O'Connor you are welcome. House of Leinster I am proud to see you within my doors." The tour was short ; as with all their activities at this period we are in ignorance of its purposes though it was probably connected with a possible French landing in Connaught.

There was little to do except wait for the French. The evening dances still went on in the Lodge and the Apothecary, " a great democrate " according to Lucy's journal, and the butcher's daughters helped out the party.

Also Lucy records that they read Volny's *Ruins*—meaning by that presumably that she and Arthur read it—and she adds severely " Arthur shock'd me by a thing he said ; he is so odd one must not judge him by other people."

IV

Suddenly the atmosphere changed, for the tremendous news came through that the French had arrived; that is to say the fleet had reached the Irish coast, but owing to the weather no landing could be made. Lord Edward and O'Connor departed immediately for Dublin. The whole quiet Kildare countryside was aroused and the capital city was in a hubbub, soldiers and militia were marching and counter-marching; the authorities were making a desperate attempt to put up some show of resistance against this, the greatest menace which ever threatened the ruling powers at the Castle. The Government scarce knew which way to turn, a powerful armament of French veterans was off the coast, commanded, it was said, by the most daring and successful young generals of the period. To meet it they had a negligible army, ill-equipped and discontent, and a militia on the loyalty of which they could not count and which in any case was merely an untrained citizen army. England at the moment could give no help, a great expeditionary force would be needed to make any impression on the French and England had to guard her own shores. Besides Pitt considered the war as lost and was making ignominious overtures for peace. On top of all this there was a far-flung and determined conspiracy within the kingdom of Ireland itself, ranging from the organised and calculating republican Presbyterians in Ulster to the desperate peasantry in Leinster and Munster. These two elements were now united in a struggle against the Castle and the days of the

Ascendancy seemed numbered. The situation looked hopeless and the Government, like a celebrated successor of later days, could only 'wait and see'.

It sometimes happens that when a cause seems lost, a second glance shows that matters are not quite so desperate. The conspiracy within the gates was, after all, not so formidable. The military commanders at Cork and Limerick sent in optimistic accounts commenting particularly on the loyalty of the people. The loyal Orange Order had grown strong in the North and could almost be relied upon on to offer full resistance to Presbyterian and Catholic United men; still the authorities feared the North most of all and an attempt to recruit militia in Belfast ended in a riot. As for Leinster and Munster, the United Irish organisation, though widespread, was not settled on a full military basis and though the peasants were brave fighting-men they were untrained and unarmed. But, more comforting than all this, it began to appear that the peasantry in the South were by no means sympathetic to the United Irish movement and a wave of loyalty to the lawful King swept over Munster. The Catholics, as in the days of the Stuarts, had an almost mystical reverence for the Sovereign, and, under threat of danger, this was intensified. Thousands of Catholic peasants joined the Yeomanry and there were 1,500 Catholics in the militia all prepared to resist the French to the death. Except in Cork, the United movement waned. To reinforce this loyal feeling, the Catholic Bishops issued strongly-worded pastorals calling on their flocks to obey their lawful monarch and governors, and—almost cynically as it would seem to us now—drawing attention to the happy Constitution under which the people lived. People were bound in conscience, the Bishops said, to assist the Government in every way against the French. The Bishop of Cork commented on the fact that " by patriotism and obedience to the established government have the Irish been distinguished even in times very different from " (what he called) " those in which we have the happiness to live ". These utterances had their effect ; and they gave great heart to the Government ; so deep was the loyal feeling in the South and West that it looked as if the French expedition would not after all have a walk-on conquest.

V

The history of the expedition—the ' Bantry Bay ' of the history-books and ballads—has been written many times and in the greatest detail, and there is a vivid account in the journals of Wolfe Tone. The whole affair with its combination of daring, frustration and petty blundering, the extraordinary intervention of the elements, the passionate impatience of Tone, and the final debacle reminds one of an episode in an ancient saga.

The endless importunity of Tone and the mission of O'Connor and Lord Edward had borne fruit. The French, to give them their due, once the matter was agreed upon, decided to do the thing in style. The chief advocate of the scheme was Lazare Hoche, a young man of thirty-six, but an experienced and incorrupt general who had distinguished himself in La Vendée. Despite the ascending star of Bonaparte, Hoche was still recognised as the French captain of the first rank. Hoche was always an advocate of the attack on Britain through Ireland, and at this period he was probably right, particularly since British naval power was so weak and diffused that there seemed no difficulty whatever in reaching the Irish coast and maintaining communications. The French force, reckoned by 18th century standards, was a large one. It consisted of seventeen ships of the line, thirteen frigates and a number of corvettes and transports making in all forty-three sail and carrying about 15,000 soldiers, as well as a large supply of arms and ammunition for distribution.

In narratives of expeditions of this kind there is a recurring phrase ' Things went wrong from the start '; the Bantry Bay enterprise went one better, things began to go wrong long before the start. Once invasion was decided upon, it was clearly desirable that the expedition should sail as soon and as secretly as possible and the Irish emissaries had emphasised that the moment was opportune for an internal rising but that it was not certain the opportunity would recur. However there was muddle in the War Ministry and muddle at the port ; Hoche, the commander on the spot, true to the tradition of military men, became so exasperated with the blundering of the Ministry that he advised the Directory to abandon the whole thing. Orders to this effect had actually been dispatched but when the messenger reached Brest he found that the fleet had sailed ; the expedition had put to sea the previous day—losing one man-o'-war and over three hundred men in the process.

After this inauspicious beginning luck held for a time. Although the season was mid-December the weather was mild and fine, and to add to the good luck the hesitancy and blundering of the British Admiralty exceeded, if anything, that of the French. The luck did not last indefinitely, within two days the winds had scattered the fleet, though there were still eighteen sail together. The missing ships included the Fraternité, and, very unwisely the commander-in-chief, General Hoche, and the Admiral both travelled on this ship. The Fraternité also carried the treasury and dispatches. It was a supreme disaster that at this early stage this important ship should be lost. She never made contact again, and so General Hoche took no further part in the expedition.

There was still a formidable armament as there had been a partial reassembly, and Grouchy—afterwards of Waterloo fame—now assumed command. The fleet, without further molestation, reached Bantry Bay.

If the full armament had landed, victory was assured. If they had landed even with the seven or eight thousand men that remained (being half the original army at Brest) the situation, in the opinion of the local commanders, would have been highly dangerous. Although we may allow for the loyalty of large sections of the peasantry and middle-class, there were signs of a United Irish rising in Munster and there was the certainty of a rising in the North, and it was understood that other French expeditions were directed to land elsewhere in Ireland. Grouchy, always intrepid, urged a landing at once, he believed that he could at least cause a diversion which would be helpful to the French and he deemed it dishonourable to return, now that the expedition had almost touched the Irish shore.

At this stage—to be precise on the 22nd Dec.—the elements interfered by way of one of those extraordinary combinations of weather which seem repeatedly to favour the British cause. In this locality, south-west of Ireland, the naturally prevailing winds come from the west or south-west. Now however, contrary to all custom the winds began to blow at gale force steadily *from the east* and continued in this point for nearly a week. The French commanders had given orders for a landing and the ships were trying to beat into Bantry harbour but after much endeavour they were unable to do so. The French Admiral, Bouvet, had taken fright; he disliked Grouchy, he had never approved of the decision to land, and was anxious to get his fleet away. He declared he did not wish to be caught in the trap of a rocky bay with a hurricane blowing. In pursuance of this policy and after giving signals which were never received, he stood out for the open sea in the flagship, leaving his fleet behind him in the bay. Once more the Admiral and the General were on the same vessel, as Grouchy was on the flagship ; and for the second time the unlucky expedition found itself without a military or a naval commander. Angry exchanges took place between the Admiral and Grouchy. Grouchy thought that he had been tricked and in this he was probably correct. The quarrel grew in intensity when the admiral took the safe but inglorious decision of returning to Brest without his fleet, bringing Grouchy like a prisoner-of-war on board. Meantime the landing within the bay was postponed. The ships rode out the gale, which blew for three whole days, accompanied now by fog and snow. In the end it was not safe to remain in the bay any longer and there had been previous discussion of diversion to the Shannon and the capture of Limerick. On the 27th December the remnant of the fleet made out to sea, and, still beating in the teeth of a furious gale, battered their way up the west coast to the Shannon. Failing to find any signs of co-operation there, the expedition returned to Brest.

So ended ' Bantry Bay '. It would be an overstatement to describe it as a fiasco. It was bravely conceived and, in part courageously executed. The expedition undoubtedly operated as a diversion and gave both the British and Irish Governments a serious fright. It gave the French some valuable information as to the practicability of a descent upon Ireland, though the pessimists in the French War Ministry still harped on the inertia of the Irish themselves. But it is important to note that many of the doubters in the French councils were converted, so much so indeed that arrangements were put in hand forthwith, this time on the Dutch coast, for a bigger and better expedition. Invasion of Ireland had become the fashion.

From the Irish patriot point of view the results were not altogether depressing. The failure of the expedition could be traced to a combination of ill-luck and muddle. What was much more serious from the United Irish standpoint was the hostility of the Munster peasantry and the feelings of loyalty evoked by danger. This gave an impetus to the conservative element in the United Irish Directory who now more than ever advocated that no rising should take place without French aid. About the North there were no doubts, but what about the rest of the country? Was it true, as subsequent historians have said, that hostility to the Castle *régime* was entirely superficial and could be remedied by comparatively small concessions, and were the United Irish wasting their time in trying to force liberty and fraternity on a stupid people who could see no further than agrarian reform? Half a century later James Fintan Lalor reminded the Young Ireland movement that the Irish would not be prevailed on to move unless stimulated by a prospect of land-division. For men who were risking life itself, for whom the spectre of the gallows was ever round the corner, these must have been serious considerations. What did Lord Edward and O'Connor think? Their subsequent actions seem to provide the answer; yet one is prompted to ask if there is anything so thankless as the task of a meliorist endeavouring to force benefits on a people who are not conscious of a want.

seventeen

I

EARLY in 1797 the Dublin executive of the Society of United Irishmen went into serious conclade. Two matters of urgent policy had to be resolved unless the movement was to split hopelessly. These were:—(1) Were they to persist in the policy of armed insurrection? and (2) If so were the United Irish to go ahead of their own accord and no longer be dependent on French aid? The first question could be disposed of, for even the most die-hard advocate of force could not oppose a last despairing appeal to the Government and the question of further French aid might not therefore arise. Thomas Addis Emmet was the outstanding advocate of every possible resort to constitutional means, while the names of Lord Edward and Arthur O'Connor were associated with the extreme party advocating force. O'Connor especially had become interested in the possibilities of the North and he thought that the restoration of Irish liberties might yet be the work of the Ulster Presbyterians. As for Lord Edward, while still favouring force, he clung to his favourite belief that if possible the Irish should conduct their own war of liberation, and admit the French, if they admitted them at all, strictly as allies. French aid was all to the good but the main thrust of the rising must be at home.

Accordingly the last overtures were made to the Opposition party to strive once more with United Irish backing to obtain the necessary reforms. The reforms asked for were in no way revolutionary, a broadening of the franchise to make it approximate to manhood suffrage, the admission of Catholics to Parliament and—most important perhaps in the circumstances—the responsibility of the Executive to Parliament ; there would follow the control of public moneys and the ending of the right of the British Privy Council to interfere in Irish affairs. Reading them now these suggested reforms are so mild that it seems incredible that a century and a half ago they should be the cause of bloodshed, or that men like Pitt and Castlereagh should have opposed them even to the extent of a civil war while their country was engaged in a desperate struggle with France.

Henry Grattan, even in this extremity, would have nothing to do with the United Irishmen, and for this attitude he has been severely criticised. It must be remembered that Grattan was a Whig, not a Liberal in the modern sense. He believed that government should be conducted honourably, fairly and judiciously, but that governmental power should rest in the hands of a class. This class comprised the owners of property. The suggestion of an extended suffrage which the United men urged, was a revolutionary principle. Emmet indeed went so far as to undertake that a message would be sent to the French that the Irish had now composed their differences with the Government and any attempt at further invasion would be opposed. Still Grattan was obdurate, he continued until 1797 to lead the Opposition in Parliament but he wished it to be understood that he was not the spokesman of the United Irish.

If Grattan had espoused their cause it is unlikely it would have made any difference, as the Government now felt itself fairly secure. Castle policy was well-calculated and secret. The chief menace lay in the North and the Government very wisely decided to concentrate on the disarming of the province of Ulster. Then by a reign of terror it was hoped to goad the rump of the United Irish in Leinster into a premature and abortive armed rising. It was a grim strategy and with the Government so resolved the year 1797 opened.

II

It will be recalled that when the French and Wolfe Tone were in Bantry Bay Lord Edward and O'Connor were in Kildare, and, as it was put laconically by Lucy, " both hastened to Dublin ". There for the moment they disappear, busily engaged in the affairs of the Leinster Executive and arranging for the expected French landing. Soon the French sailed away and the Executive had to face a new situation, but O'Connor was more than ever persuaded that their chief hope now rested with the Societies of the North. Accordingly he made arrangements for a visit by himself and Lord Edward to that province.

In December '96 the little party in Kildare had, for different reasons broken up. Before this happened they had a visit from Lord and Lady Castlereagh. The Castlereaghs brought a message from Castletown that aunt Henrietta was ill, and Lucy was asked to go at once and if possible to stay with her. This did not fit in with Lucy's plans at all. Lord Edward and Arthur had just settled to go to Dublin and Arthur was to go on to Belfast to present the *Address to the People of Antrim* upon which he had been working and which was now nearly ready. There was nothing more to be done at the moment so Lucy, rather reluctantly, went to Castletown.

o

When the news came that the French had left, Arthur
wrote to Lucy asking her to accompany them on the
Northern journey. Naturally Lucy was all excitement and
was eager to go, but Pamela advised against it, and, after
much persuasion by the aunts, Lucy tearfully decided to
stay. Eventually Arthur O'Connor went alone, and the
Address to the People of Antrim appeared in the *Northern
Star* in January. Lord Edward then went to Belfast, and
the two leaders spent some time in discussions with the
United leaders in that city. By Jan. 21st Lord Edward
was back in Kildare, and Lucy, all impatience at Castletown, arranged to go over the following day to hear the
latest about Arthur. Together she and Lord Edward
read the *Address*, she with pride mingled with anxiety.
They all knew at this time that the Government was ready
to take action, and warnings were daily coming from
their influential friends and even from the Castle. A few
days later, on Feb. 3rd, the first blow fell. Arthur O'Connor was arrested while walking with Lord Edward in
Dublin and was lodged in Newgate. Lucy visited him
every day, that is to say he appeared at a window
and waved to the friends outside, and he wrote long and
dolorous letters to her. Six months later he was released
without trial, (the Habeas Corpus Act was suspended) and
shortly afterwards resumed his activities with the United
Irishmen.

In March Lord Edward, Pamela and Lucy went to
Frescati which once again was vacant, While the worries
of the family increased, Lord Edward continued to receive the United Irish leaders there. All this time
his mother was in England, but his half-sister
Cecilia Ogilvie wrote to say how anxious the Duchess was.
This determined Lord Edward to go across and see her
and he informed Lucy that he was going to take her to
England. She protested and pleaded, but when told that
the Duchess was ill, and that the trip was only a visit,

she agreed to go. They crossed in May but Lord Edward soon returned, leaving Lucy behind in England. It was the last time he saw his mother.

III

Irish affairs were going from bad to worse. Parliament had met on the 16th January under the shadow of a new liability, for England was now at war with Spain and the Castle Government had an excuse to augment the Yeomanry. The Government decision to subdue Ulster has already been referred to ; this led to the campaign which is known in history as the Disarming of the North. This operation was important in many ways. It was the first real taste of a reign of terror conducted by undisciplined Yeomanry and Orangemen. Also it demonstrated the effectiveness of terrorism in countering preparations for a rising or alternatively in provoking hopeless resistance. But most of all the disarming broke the back of the United Irish movement, and from the moment it was effective all hope of a successful rebellion disappeared. It is true that the United men in Belfast and adjacent areas stood firm and were ready when the call came, but the network of the organisation in the other Ulster counties was rooted out, and the burnings and pillagings caused arms to be surrendered in terror, while the sad fate of William Orr showed that juries were prepared to condemn a man to death on doubtful evidence merely for having administered an unlawful ' test '.

Apart from Belfast and the Northern area, the United Irish Society had no effective organisation except in Dublin, the two Meaths and Kildare; although impressive figures could be given to Lord Edward, if he called for them, as to the strength of the organisation. After the Northern disarming it was evident that the rising when

it came would be a partial affair, a disorganised effort in
which the Jacobinism of the North would be mixed up
with the religious resentment and petty agrarianism of the
South.

The Government was now keeping a close eye on
Lord Edward, for by mid-1797 their informers could tell
them definitely that he was the intended commander-in-
chief of the insurgent army. He was no longer regarded as
an irresponsible young follower of Tom Paine, but was
recognised as a man of energy and daring with considerable
military experience and talent,. However much Lord
Clare might persist in regarding Lord Edward as a criminal hothead, the man was now a great danger to the
established order and Castlereagh and some others began
pressing that he should either be arrested or driven to
flee the country. Lord Robert Fitzgerald, Edward's
junior brother, was Minister in Copenhagen and he
offered Edward asylum in the British Embassy there, and
later he tendered his resignation to the king. George III
refused to accept on the grounds that " a good brother
could not be a bad Minister." But this offer of asylum
was no more acceptable than were Ogilvie's pleas for
flight, though Ogilvie travelled specially to Dublin to
make his plea in person.

The information which the Government was daily
receiving was growing very serious, especially as pointing
to Lord Edward. He decided not to stand for Parliament
in the election of 1797 and instead he issued an *Address
to the People of Kildare*. During 1797 he made a secret
trip to London to meet a Swede named Jagerhorn who
was a French agent. There is no record that even his
mother knew of this trip, but we can rest assured that it
did not pass unnoticed by the authorities either at home
or in England, for at this time there was a notorious Irish
informer named Turner operating in Hamburg who
notified the British authorities of the proposed meeting.

He also conveyed the interesting news that there was a " female friend " of Lord Edward through whom correspondence was maintained with France. This " friend " must have been Pamela. There was also the affair of Watty Cox. Cox was a broken-down journalist and afterwards an informer. He had started up a broadsheet in Dublin called the *Union Star*, advocating assassination as a policy. Afterwards he said that O'Connor and Lord Edward were implicated in this policy, an allegation hotly denied by O'Connor. There is no doubt that Lord Edward and O'Connor had some association with Cox and the affair convinced the Government that Lord Edward was the leading spirit in the " physical force " party in the United movement. It was felt that if he could be got out of the way the military organisation—at least in Leinster—would collapse. This was true ; O'Connor the other great activist was already under lock and key and he was presently to be charged with sedition, possibly with treason. The Government advisers saw however that there was no available evidence against him and, as stated, O'Connor was released in August 1797. Lord Edward might also have been arrested around this time but the Castle junta was in a dilemma. More than once it was decided that things had gone far enough and that a swoop could be made. Why was this step not taken ?

If the leaders had been arrested in 1797 there would have been no rising in 1798. Further, the fact that the organisation was almost broken by the disarming in Ulster, and that elsewhere the leaders were dispersed, might have caused the French seriously to reconsider their policy of invasion. It was difficult enough to induce the French to act even by representing that the whole country was waiting to rise, and it may be presumed that they would abandon a landing in a hostile country. In favour of the Government it is urged that there were legal difficulties in the way of obtaining convictions owing to reluctance of informers to give evidence and their fear of assassination. This need not have worried the Castle as the Habeas Corpus Act was suspended ; without any legal risk the leaders could be kept in custody for a year or so until the immediate crisis blew over. Indeed sufficient evidence might be forthcoming to convict most of them in the ordinary legal course. It surely was the first duty of a Government to take proper steps at this juncture to secure the safety of the people and the realm. It would have been easy to do so and the question is asked : why did not the Government act?

The answer usually given is that the policy of both the British and Irish Governments was to drive the people into rebellion, to crush the rebellion with terror and slaughter, and so facilitate the legislative Union. A legislative union was more than a mere union of Parliaments, for it implied the destruction of the independent Kingdom.

Much has been written about this grave indictment, but an examination would take us too far away from the present narrative. It may be said, however, that on the evidence the charge is probably sustained.

eighteen

I

BY the end of the year 1797 the pressure of the active party within the ranks of the United Irish had become insistent, and there were frequent calls for an immediate rising. Hitherto the movement was local in character but now the organisation was widespread and there was an attempt to organise on a national scale. An all-Ireland convention was held secretly in Dublin and this gathering passed two noteworthy resolutions. Firstly it was decided to abandon any further attempt to parley with the Parliamentary opposition or to confine the movement to constitutional activity. The second resolution was an appeal to certain areas which had become particularly restive and were calling loudly for hostilities. The list of these counties indicates the places where the organisation was best advanced or where repression was especially brutal ; the counties were Carlow, Meath and Wicklow in Leinster, and Antrim, Down and Derry in Ulster.

Lord Edward and the active party were resolute on an insurrection, with or without French aid, and it was accordingly agreed to let them have their way. In January of 1798 therefore a ' military committee ' was formed which got down forthwith to detailed preparations, and the first step was to constitute Lord Edward as formal commander-in-chief—the conservative wing, whatever their misgivings, loyally decided to cooperate fully. Lord Edward was overflowing with optimism, and an interesting dialogue is preserved which illustrates the type of objection which was being made by the conservatives. Lord Edward claimed to have 100,000 men enrolled and ready to join the ranks of the insurgents, and he could produce detailed figures. His interrogator pointed out that this meant 50,000 men in the field—if indeed that number—most of them undisciplined and unarmed. We would need, he went on, at least 15,000 French. Lord Edward replied that they might not get any French soldiers and he was told that they should at least try to get some French officers. His interrogator, who seems to have been a shrewd man, stressed the lesson which is learned by so many revolutionaries ; how little avail is enthusiasm or manpower against discipline and arms. But Lord Edward cried down every objection and events marched to the climax.

It seems pertinent to enquire whether there was any ground for his optimism. It is difficult now to appraise a situation in which there were so many uncertain elements, of which one outstanding uncertainty was the attitude of the people. Some historians claim that, but for the initial arrests, the rising would have succeeded in over-throwing the existing order, and British power in Ireland—temporarily at least—would have disappeared. On the other hand there is little doubt that the British, thoroughly frightened of the French, would in the last resort have thrown in great military resources rather than let the country fall into the hands of French allies. This may be inferred from the decision to send the great army which was mustered to crush a puny French expedition at Killala.

On the factual side of military numbers there seems no justification for Lord Edward's boyish enthusiasm.

The counties of Antrim and Down and parts of other areas in the North were still organised and well disciplined, the men were earnest and brave, there was a well-trained nucleus and they might count on the defection of the militia. Yet the number of United Irishmen actually in readiness to turn out was small. It must not be forgotten that the disarming of Ulster and the reign of terror had its effect. Moreover ugly dissensions had now appeared in the Ulster ranks, many Ulstermen feared that should the Castle regime be overthrown a Roman Catholic oligarchy would be operating in Dublin. With the traditional Presbyterian fear of clericalism they asked themselves, not without reason, whether they would not be worse off in the end. As for the other provinces there are no reliable figures, all that we can do is to judge by results. Connaught and Munster did not rise at all, and the great rising in Wexford was, as it were, an afterthought.

These developments produced a parallel excitement in the Castle and there the old controversy was revived: should they strike now or allow matters to ripen further. The British Government, it will be recalled, as late as the winter of 1797 was still counselling a policy of waiting, but early in 1798 the Castle, thanks to a great network of spies and informers, was able to make new and more pressing representations. The formation of the military committee was urged as the immediate step to civil war, but even then the British held back. In the end it was the fear of French invasion, not of Irish rebellion, that was the deciding factor, and the information came, not out of Ireland, but from British spies in Paris and elsewhere. Pitt was convinced that a new and great expeditionary force would soon be at the coasts of Ireland. The Irish authorities emphasised that just at the present moment it would be easy to deal a destructive blow to the United organisation. They represented the movement as a small nucleus of clever and devoted men in Dublin and Belfast, with a great following of undisciplined and unarmed peasantry which would melt away when the leaders were removed. What more simple than to arrest the leaders? This, they pointed out, could easily be done under existing powers. Martial law could then be declared for the whole country and the yeomanry and militia—not to speak of the Orangemen—would soon deal with any disturbances in the provinces. No military action as such was involved. These arguments, coupled with the imminent fear of invasion, impressed the British cabinet and word was given to proceed.

Fate, as always, seemed to favour the Castle for just at the right moment a kind of super-informer came forward. He was actually a member of the Leinster Directory which now operated as a National Committee, since, with the exception of the Ulstermen, all societies in the provinces were represented. The difficulty in the Castle was not to get informers who would give valuable information, but to get one who would be willing to come forward and testify in court. So far no agent would agree to do this; but now, by an extraordinary stroke of luck, the Castle found Thomas Reynolds.

Reynolds was a distant relative of Lord Edward himself. He had been a merchant in Dublin and had gone bankrupt but he had an ambition to be a country gentleman, acceptable to the county and keeping an especially good cellar. Such things require money, and he had taken the first step towards his goal when, through the good offices of Lord Edward, he obtained a lease of Kilkea Castle, one of the Leinster properties in Kildare. He was thus a neighbour of Lord Edward and he held high rank in the county organisation of the United Irishmen. To give him his due, he seems to have had a genuine liking for Lord Edward and this made the role of traitor rather difficult; but still money had to be found for the cellars of Kilkea, and the Castle paid handsomely. Capacity for self-deception is illimitable and like many informers he persuaded himself that he was acting in the public good. He probably had not read Dante who had such a horror of treachery that he consigned traitors to the lowest pit of the Inferno, lower even than that of the murderers.

Fate sided further with the Government since it was arranged that a plenary session of the whole Leinster Directory would soon be held in Dublin. At one swoop they could all be arrested and this would be simpler than piecemeal execution of warrants. The authorities asked Reynolds to keep them informed and it was ascertained that this fateful meeting would take place in the house of Oliver Bond in Bridge street on a day, memorable in Irish history—12th March, 1798—and that the entire Directory would be present. Reynolds seems to have repented somewhat of this desperate betrayal, for he waited at Leinster House and warned Lord Edward, pretending that he had information from the Castle, and Lord Edward did not, in consequence, attend the meeting. A raid was duly carried out at Bond's and thirteen leaders and some others were captured.

Lord Edward not being present, a warrant was issued and the picket went to Leinster House, but the quarry, being warned, escaped at the rear via the stables. In charge of a Captain Kelly, the picket carried out a search and by all accounts behaved with courtesy. Pamela was indisposed, being advanced in pregnancy, but the captain nevertheless entered and searched her room. Here we meet with another instance of the almost inexcusable carelessness of the United Irish leaders. In a writing bureau in Pamela's room the captain came across nothing less than a detailed memorandum on street fighting and a plan for an attack on Dublin—all in Lord Edward's handwriting. Indeed Lord Edward seems to have had a weakness for drawing up documents of the most incriminating kind in his own handwriting, and then disposing of them carelessly. Reynolds the informer tells of a meeting of United leaders which he had attended on the previous 24th of February at Frescati during which with other things plans for a military rising were discussed. Lord Edward had drafted a report of the numerical strength of the United forces in the counties, once again, to be sure, in his own hand, and then passed this precious document on to Reynolds. That evening it was in Dublin Castle.

Not finding their man, the picket withdrew. It was evening, and meanwhile Lord Edward had made his way to a hideout in Mount Jerome, near the house of John Keogh the Catholic leader. In the gathering darkness he may have turned to take a last look at the great mansion, and his thoughts were centred upon his beloved wife and the coming of their third child. Though his reflections were bitter he was cheered by the imminent excitements of a nation-wide rising, but little did he think that never again would he set foot within the splendid apartments of Leinster House.

II

The news of the arrests caused consternation. People did not know exactly what to believe. Unconcsiously the Government had made a dramatic and telling gesture— the entire Directory surprised and arrested while actually in session! The moral value was great, even if not immediately recognised, for there were ceaseless rumours of worse things to come, and a sense of hopelessness swept through many sections of the United Irish movement. Even Government supporters were surprised; some at the thorough *coup*, some at the extent of the conspiracy.

But the Castle victory was by no means complete. Though some of the United Irishmen were disheartened, the active party, or what remained of it, seemed to have gathered new inspiration. The prevailing cry was " Stand firm and fill the breaches ". Also, though the captures were extensive, some of the more effective leaders were still at liberty, notably, of course, Lord Edward. Arthur O 'Connor had departed on his second mission to France, but two other leaders now assumed prominence, the ill-fated brothers John and Henry Sheares. John Sheares favoured an attempt to win over the military and he also had faith in the potential of Munster, particularly of Co. Cork.

The authorities saw that they would have to take further measures. The arrest of some of the leaders was not enough, particularly with Lord Edward at large. Accordingly martial law for the whole country was proclaimed on the 20th of March. This was a frightful measure of repression for it removed the legal shackles, such as they were, from the activities of the yeomen and militia, and it enabled the military authorities to act then and there without the intervention of the civil magistrate. To the Castle junta it gave what amounted to absolute power. The history of this dreadful period has been written many times, the horrors of the pitch-cap and the half-hangings, the looting, burning and raping, the exploits of Lieutenant Hepenstall the ' walking gallows ' who used to hang men on his back, and a thousand other atrocities. This is not the place to set them out again or to chronicle the 1798 Rising. A maddened peasantry particularly in Leinster could with difficulty be restrained from massacre while from the disciplined ranks of the United men in Ulster came daily appeals, French or no French, to fix the date for the rising.

Lord Edward, meanwhile, was moving stealthily in disguise round the suburbs of Dublin. To him the

United leaders deferred, and on his shoulders fell the direction of reorganisation in face of martial law. So great was the enthusiasm that it is said that within four days the vacant seats on the Directory were filled. It was arranged that, for the present, Lord Edward should remain concealed in Dublin, undertaking an occasional tour of Leinster for discussions and review. All through the month of April this arrangement was followed.

nineteen

I

ON the southwest confines of the city, in the district now called Portobello, the fields and open countryside swept right up to the canal. It was a bright and healthy locality, favoured by prevailing westerly winds blowing from the country, and the picturesque canal harbour may have given the district its name. At the canal lock there is the fine structure of the hotel built to accommodate passengers on the canal boats. A little to the westward of this mansion on the same side was the humble dwelling of a certain Widow Dillon, and the little house was standing until the end of the last century.

Here for some weeks the fugitive commander-in-chief set up a sort of headquarters. Escaping from Leinster House he went to Mount Jerome, but this was remote, and the next move was to the house of a good friend, a Dr. Kennedy, in Aungier St. for a short stay, and then to the Widow Dillon's. The move to Dr. Kennedy's was partly for what we should now call observation, for Lord Edward's health was declining under the strain. He was sustained by hope and excitement exhilarated by the pending conflict, yet his sufferings and anxieties were great. He was a fugitive, and if arrested he knew not what his fate might be. He was anxious as ever about his mother and the family, particularly perhaps about Lucy and his well-loved brother Lord Henry. Above all he was thinking of Pamela and the child soon to be born. He heard stories that the authorities were worrying Pamela and that she was ordered to leave the country forthwith. She had left Leinster House and taken a furnished house in Denzille Street, and he determined at all hazards to see her at once. He did succeed in visiting her unexpectedly, in disguise, one evening at dusk, and the shock was so great that she had a premature confinement.

The tension of this way of life was telling on his constitution, naturally robust and vigourous. Hardship he did not mind, provided it was outdoor and active ; but creeping by night about wretched purlieus, this confinement during the bracing springtime weather, this neverending vigilance and murmur of hushed voices, all were things that preyed on him. It was a great relief to set off with his lieutenant, Sam Neilson, for a tour of Kildare and Carlow to organise the societies for action in these areas and give final directions for the rising. It was dangerous also, but not so dangerous in those days of primitive communications as it seems to us now. Nonetheless the pair, although disguised, had some narrow escapes from military patrols.

Sam Neilson, the faithful Sam, was acting as liaison officer and deputy just now. This woollen-draper from Belfast, unwieldly of body and slow of thought, was not a man of great intellect, but he had something like veneration for Lord Edward. He was now middle-aged, had sacrificed much, and was above all incorruptible. With these high qualities he combined the impulsiveness of adolescence which made him a dangerous *aide* for Lord Edward to have about his person. There are examples of this later, and the indiscretions are so annoying as to have laid Neilson open to the charge of treachery. At the moment he was the principal *aide-de-camp*.

So the month passed at Portobello. Lord Edward lay quiet by day, and after dark he went for walks along the canal bank. By day someone in the house was always on the alert for pickets touring the neighbourhood and listening apprehensively to every knock at the door. It was a wearying interlude.

At this time the Fitzgerald family (except Lord Edward's brother the Duke) were in England, living at the Duchess's house in Harley Street. There the news of the Irish arrests was received with the greatest anxiety. Lord Edward, the beloved Eddy, was a fugitive from justice, wanted on a charge of high treason. Something must be done at once, for it was known that the Government had decided to proceed against the State Prisoners— as the imprisoned leaders were called—on charges of treason ; there seemed to be little that could arrest judgement, and the punishment for treason was not only hanging and quartering but also forfeiture of property. There was therefore utter panic in Harley Street and an urgent family council was held. There were powerful friends in high places but there was little that could be done at the moment. Eventually it was decided that Ogilvie should set out for Ireland.

That hard-headed Scotsman had always opposed Lord Edward's political activities and would have been entitled to adopt an " I-told-you-so " attitude. To his credit, and probably out of feeling for Emily, he now acted generously. It was settled as an immediate plan of action that Ogilvie should go to Dublin and get in touch with Lord Edward and persuade him to leave the country. His mission may appear to have been hopeless, but actually he had something tangible to offer. Lady Louisa Conolly was, it may be recalled, a great friend of Lord Chancellor Clare and Castlereagh the Chief Secretary, and Castlereagh and his wife were frequent visitors at Castletown. Lady Louisa had approached both Clare and

P

Castlereagh, her request being that her misguided but beloved nephew be allowed to escape. The reply was gratifying. Both the Chancellor and Castlereagh hastened to say that they were only too willing to facilitate the flight. This may seem generous, in reality it was good business for the authorities; the Castle was really alarmed for they heard that an insurrection was planned in a matter of weeks and Pitt had reports that two great French expeditions were assembling at the Texel and Le Havre. It was high time to put the kingdom in order.

Armed with this undertaking the optimist Ogilvie journeyed to Dublin, remembering how tearfully his wife had begged him to do his utmost. He managed to make contact with Lord Edward at the Widow Dillon's and elsewhere and had some long and earnest arguments. As might be expected his entreaties were vain. Edward respected Ogilvie, but not even that most telling of arguments, the mortal anxiety of his dear mother, could move him. He would not think of abandoning his post, now that the final arrangements were made for the insurrection. There was nothing for the step-father to do but report his failure to Aunt Louisa and return sorrowfully to London.

II

Ogilvie's errand however had one definite result. The Castle resolved to give up trifling, and, now that their quarry would not take his chance to escape, they determined to have him dead or alive. The man-hunt would be redoubled. It was already the month of May and the rising, they heard, was fixed for that month. There was no time to lose. Ogilvie departed and a day or two later a proclamation was posted up all over Dublin offering £1000 for the capture of Lord Edward Fitzgerald. The results were swift and decisive.

The net was closing and the pursuit was intensified. The authorities had plenty of informers and they traced Lord Edward to the Widow's and thence to the district known as the Liberties. There was however great difficulty at first in getting an informer to betray the actual hiding-place of the Geraldine; no one, it seemed, was sufficiently hardened for this. In the circumstances, Lord Edward had to leave Portobello and the kindly comforts of Mrs. Dillon and for a time he found refuge in a number of houses in the Liberties, chiefly in the High Street-Thomas Street area. He went first to Murphy, a feather-merchant in Thomas Street, then to Cormack's in the same street, then to Moore's in Thomas Street, then to a linen draper's house, Gannon's in High Street, and finally back to Murphy's. The Government knew well that he was moving about these streets at night, and, at length, thanks to the thousand-pounds reward, they had made contact with a reliable informer close to the person of Lord Edward. This gentleman though in the inner confidence of the fugitive, seemed always just a day late with his information and the Castle was getting impatient.

Important decisions had meantime been taken by the United men; the date of the rising had been fixed for May 24th, there was less than a week to go ; Lord Edward's brilliant green and gold uniform had already been delivered. The pikes were distributed throughout the counties. The safety of the commander-in-chief became doubly important and the indiscreet Sam Neilson took on the direction of affairs. A sort of bodyguard was formed which preceded and followed Lord Edward whenever he had to make a nightly sally through the streets—not, one would imagine an ideal way of concealment ; indeed the well-meaning attentions of Sam were proving a serious embarrassment.

So we come to Friday, 18th May. It was arranged that on the evening of this day Lord Edward once again should go to Murphy's. As an instance of how close the authorities were on his tracks Lord Edward (with the inevitable bodyguard) had been waylaid the previous evening by a picket at the lower end of Watling street. The Castle had got direct information as to the route, and for once the escort proved useful ; Major Sirr, the police officer, not anticipating a bodyguard, unwisely omitted to bring sufficient force. The result was a street *fracas* and it is said that Major Sirr actually grappled with Lord Edward, but was himself assaulted in turn, and Lord Edward, much shaken, got away. Late that night, exhausted and ill, he arrived at Murphy's.

The following day, Saturday, Lord Edward was partially refreshed after his rest, but his health was now definitely bad and he was suffering from some sort of chronic cold. His appearance was drawn and haggard but his spirits were buoyant. The hunt continued mercilessly and it was clear that the Liberties area was hopeless as a place of concealment; it had in fact been arranged that Lord Edward should move next day to a refuge in Sandymount. That Saturday morning, the pickets raided the house where he had been only the previous day, and the soldiers even halted doubtfully outside Murphy's. The Castle party was urging Sirr to the utmost efforts and the latter was in hourly contact with the informer. The unfortunate Murphy in great trepidation, peered through his windows at the raiding-pickets nearby, for he knew not what disasters might befall him if Lord Edward was discovered on his premises. He took the green-and-gold uniform and hid it in a loft; and he urged Lord Edward during the day to take refuge in a valley between the rooftops so that he could escape over the roofs. To add to poor Murphy's discomfort the faithful Sam Neilson was early on the scene to safeguard the chief as he thought ; but in reality he added to the danger by marching up and down outside and scrutinising those approaching the house.

The raiding-parties departed about midday and the street became normal. Murphy ventured to ask Lord Edward to come down from his perch in the roof-valley to dinner. He dined about four o'clock with Sam Nielson for company and immediately afterwards Nielson departed, a fact which afterwards was used in allegations of treachery for which there was no foundation.

III

Sirr and his party arrived in the late afternoon empty-handed at the Castle. There they made immediate contact again with the informer and the message received was the fatal one: ' go *at once* to the house of Murphy the feather-merchant in Thomas St., Lord Edward being there at this very minute.' No time was lost, the pickets set out and an order was sent to the patrols in the neighbourhood to converge on Murphy's.

Meantime in that establishment dinner was over and Neilson had departed. Lord Edward, still in ill-health went to his attic room and lay on the bed, his pistols nearby, while beside him on the bed was a long double-edged dagger with a villainous waved blade of a pattern manufactured for the United Irishmen. He rested for an hour or two. Then about seven o'clock his host Murphy went up to ask if he would come down to tea. While Murphy was in the room rapid footsteps were heard on the stairs and before either could recover from his start, Major Swan, a magistrate, entered the room— alone, it seems, at first. He moved towards Lord Edward with pistol drawn and said "You are my prisoner". Murphy attempted to obstruct but received a blow of the pistol under the eye which inflicted a nasty wound. Lord Edward was reclining on the bed when Swan entered, but, springing instantly to his feet, he struck at Swan with the dagger inflicting slight wounds on the hands. Swan attempted to fire the pistol but it misfired, and setting up a howl that he was murdered he called on his companion, a Captain Ryan, to come to his aid.

The raiding-party consisted of Town-Major Sirr and a posse of military, Town-Major Swan the magistrate, and Captain Ryan. This Captain Ryan was a militia officer—hence the title—and had made it a habit latterly to volunteer his services on these pickets, doubtless with a view to gaining attention at the Castle. By profession he was a journalist with a proprietary interest in some journals of the time. Whatever one may think of his political opinions and time-serving, his conduct on the present occasion shows that he was a brave man.

To return to the scene in the chamber, Ryan, armed only with a sword-cane rushed to the aid of Swan, pushed Murphy, who was bleeding severely, out into the passage, and immediately grappled with Lord Edward. Swan meantime rushed down the stairs, again shouting that he was murdered. In the room a desperate and horrifying struggle took place. Ryan on grappling with Lord Edward received a deep wound from the dagger in the stomach but he forced his antagonist backwards on the bed. There the two men rolled over spattered with blood, Lord Edward fighting with the frenzy of a maniac. Fourteen times in all he plunged that vicious dagger into Ryan's body until the viscera of that officer were protruding. Lord Edward jumped up, again attempting to make for the door. Ryan, no longer being able to grasp him with his arms, rolled from the bed to the floor and held on to Lord Edward with his legs.

This deadly struggle went on for nearly ten minutes and there seems to have been some inexplicable delay on Major Sirr's part in not bringing his posse of military to the rescue. Once again Lord Edward raised the dagger to strike at the prostrate Ryan, but Major Sirr at last was at the door and seeing how things were going he took aim with his pistol at the dagger arm and wounded Lord Edward near the right shoulder. The dagger dropped from his hand but even then he was determined to resist to the last. Blood now streamed from his shoulder where the pistol ball was lodged, he was weak with pain yet he made one last effort to gain the door. Sirr signalled the military to enter, and, crossing their muskets, they forced Lord Edward backwards on the floor, one of them inflicting another wound in his neck in the process. Lord Edward, exhausted and over-powered, was secured and bound; a surgeon, who happened to be in a nearby house, was called in and gave first aid to the wounded; Lord Edward, faint and exhausted was borne in a sedan-chair to the Castle, heavily guarded.

IV

At the Castle, strangely enough, Lord Edward was received not as a dangerous revolutionary who had just half-murdered an officer while resisting arrest, but rather as something of an honoured guest. Quite a fuss was made. It was of course a tremendous capture, and in those days Lord Edward's social rank and position as well as his powerful connections in England and Ireland required that he be treated with especial ceremony. We are told that Camden the Lord Lieutenant was overcome with emotion when the news was brought and sent his own secretary to assure the captive that he would have every attention. Meantime the Surgeon-General himself, Stewart, had also been summoned and dressed the wound with his own hands and pronounced it not dangerous. It was intended that the captive should be detained as a military prisoner at the Castle—martial law was then in force—but the civil authority represented by the magist-rates stepped in. On the ground that in resisting arrest he had wounded agents of the civil power, they demanded that he be delivered up and sent to the common gaol at Newgate. To Newgate therefore he was taken. His last and only message to the Secretary was a request to break the news gently to his wife Pamela; that lady, despite her recent premature confinement was attending a party at Lady Moira's and did not get the news until the following morning.

twenty

I

LORD Edward's friend Arthur O'Connor was having adventures scarcely less dramatic. In February, 1798, O'Connor had set out for London again *en route* for France. Lewins, the United Irish representative in Paris, was sending pessimistic reports, and the need for an immediate expedition was never greater. The sending of three seperate expeditions was already decided in principle, but the delays were fatal. O'Connor's task was to see that the expeditions set out.

He reached London and, in anticipation of dangers ahead, was determined to have a gay time. As on the previous occasion he met his friends the Whig leaders and exchanged congenial opinions about the evils of government both in England and Ireland. Whether he disclosed his purpose in visiting France to Charles James Fox must remain in doubt, but if he did, Fox apparently did not disapprove. Despite Ogilvie's hostility, O'Connor dined at Harley Street and made an effort to keep the conversation clear of the troubles in Ireland. Lucy of course was in a state of wild excitement. She was sure now that she was in love, but, she says, having pondered the matter deeply she came to the conclusion not to marry Arthur O'Connor. Marriage and world-betterment do not go easily together, and the romance, if she only knew it, was indeed drawing to an end.

There was no time to be lost, pleasant as was this gay and intellectual society in London. O'Connor was to have three companions, two were camp-followers, but the third, a silenced priest named Coigley (or Quigley) deserves some mention. He had long been identified with the revolutionary movement, having been inclined that way by the Orange atrocities in his native county of Louth, and had got into trouble with his superiors. He had already been in France and was also in touch with the small coterie of English revolutionaries in London. On account of this English connection he was a dangerous companion, for O'Connor was putting up the case that he was going abroad to escape from debt. The Castle of course knew of the mission, but they were not sorry to see O'Connor leave the country.

II

On a bleak February afternoon in the year 1798 just as dark was setting in four men arrived at the fishing village of Margate on the Kent coast. Their arrival caused some comment as they had a great amount of luggage which they pushed before them, pilgrim fashion, on a hand-cart. Two of the gentlemen were well-spoken and authoritative the other two were more humble. They put up for the night at the King's Head Hotel. Their stay in Margate was short. The following morning Bow Street officers arrived, took all four into custody and made a search of the premises and luggage. In the pocket of the overcoat of one of the travellers they found nothing less than a message of congratulation to General Bonaparte who had just concluded a victorious campaign in Italy. The message also went on to say that his friends in England had only one wish, namely to see the hero of Italy and his invincible legions landed on the English coast.

The four travellers were Arthur O'Connor and James Coigley, and two others named Allen and Leary who stated that they were servants. They were put on trial at Maidstone, charged with the capital offence of treason.

The trial of the four men was remarkable in many respects. Whether the verdict is a tribute to the credulity of an English jury or to the fairness of English law must be a matter of opinion. There was much hard swearing. The case also illustrates the difficulty of that legal requirement known as proof, for treason in the ill-defined state of the law was by no means an easy offence to prove home, and English juries were disinclined to punish men for what they regarded as crimes of opinion.

Arthur O'Connor and his three associates were charged as stated with High Treason, an unusual offence in England in modern times. O'Connor was a well-known Irish revolutionary, but this was not relevant evidence. His defence appeared weak, he declared that he was going to France on private business and not on any political mission, but despite the secrecy of his departure it was difficult to disprove this. Coigley, however, was in a much worse position, for it was in his pocket that the officers had found a paper which was definitely treasonable. His defence was scarcely less remarkable than O'Connor's. He said that he had no knowledge of the invitation to Bonaparte. Asked to account for the paper, he said that it must have been 'planted' there either by the Bow Street officers or by some enemy. The jury, not surprisingly, did not believe this.

The trial took a further unexpected turn when O'Connor called a whole gallery of celebrities to testify as to his character and loyal disposition. The fact that they all made the journey to Margate—some even crossing from

Ireland—is a measure of the popularity and influence of O'Connor. The list of names makes impressive reading : Lord Moira, the Hon. Thomas Erskine, Right Hon. Charles James Fox, the Earl of Suffolk, Rt. Hon. Richard Brinsley Sheridan, Rt. Hon. Henry Grattan, Lord John Russell, Lord Thanet and Lord Oxford. These gentlemen attended to testify—in rebuttal of a treason charge—that O'Connor bore loyal and affectionate sentiments towards His Majesty and the established order. It may be that the cross-examination by the prosecution was half-hearted, or it may be that the noble lords and gentlemen giving evidence salved their consciences in ambiguity. Mr. Fox, for example said that he believed Arthur O'Connor to be highly enlightened and firmly attached to the principles which seated the present family on the throne, to which principles they owed their liberty. This can be read in more senses than one. Brinsley Sheridan, wisely for once, insisted that O'Connor's political opinions related only to Ireland and he also said that he never met any man who more repudiated the idea of any part of England requiring French assistance. Henry Grattan, struggling with difficulties, said that he "never imagined" O'Connor would favour an invasion of his country.

The jury may well have quailed before this barrage of distinguished tribute. With sound commonsense however, they drew the distinction between treason in England and the same offence in Ireland. These men were Irish revolutionaries—the jury must have been satisfied as to that— they were on their way to France to seek aid to overthrow the present Irish regime. Amongst the common people of England there was no great love for the Irish Government and its doings. Strange stories came across the Channel about oppression and murder and the imminence of rebellion. There was little or no evidence that O'Connor and two of his associates Leary and Allen had plotted against Britain, and the jury brought in a verdict of

' Not Guilty ' in their favour. But with every good-will the jury could not overlook the document found on the unfortunate Coigley. This letter had been issued by a ' Secret Committee in England ' associated with one or two well-known Correspondence Societies in London. He was found guilty and sentenced to be hanged. The three others were acquitted.

When the verdicts were brought in there was an exciting scene in the court. O'Connor and the others, considering themselves free men rushed to leave the court. But there was present a party of officers, armed with a warrant signed by Portland the Secretary of State, for the re-arrest of O'Connor on another charge of High Treason. One would have though that this was *res judicata* but the Castle apparently was at work and wished to have O'Connor put on trial in Ireland where his fate no doubt would be different. He was therefore re-arrested and removed to Dublin where he shared the imprisonment of the so-called State Prisoners. Coigley was executed on the following day.

This re-arrest effectively terminated Arthur O'Connor's activities in Irish affairs. He was kept in prison until the Peace of Amiens in 1802 and then sent into exile. The remainder of his long life (he died aged 92) belongs to France, where, surviving revolution and counter-revolution, he married a daughter of Condorcet, and rose to be a general in the French army. As for Lucy, he saw little of her after the Maidstone trial. That spirited young lady, perhaps to console herself for sorrows and disappointments in Ireland, entered into the distractions of London society, particularly at Holland House, and in the witty circle of that famous establishment she held her own. She had an aptitude for falling in love, and it was not long before she had new admirers. There was a Mr. Marsh, a clergyman to whom the Duchess objected because he was poor. Mr. Marsh was thereby saved unhappiness for he had a dread of what he called " French Principles ". The times were dark and evil. Everywhere he looked, the poor man saw sinister evidence of the disease he knew as 'democracy', and his life was miserable in consequence. At times he believed he even detected symptoms of democracy in the opinions of his loved one and he attributed this to the notorious lack of intelligence in women.

Mr. Marsh was disposed of, and four years later Lucy married a Captain Foley who was afterwards promoted admiral. She lived chiefly on her husband's estates in Wales. She was childless, but she had a long and happy life, dying in the south of France at the age of eighty, and retaining her high spirits and her interest in ' deomcracy ' to the end.

III

A last word may be said about the Maidstone business. The trial aroused greater interest in England than was anticipated, and in some respects the Government felt uncomfortable. There was a novel and critical concern with Irish conditions. There was a feeling that the misgovernment across the water derived from conspiracy between certain ruling-classes in England and Ireland and that the true state of affairs was concealed. Coigley for a time was a Whig hero, though it must be said that not all the Whigs shared the view. As an illustration there is the retort of Dr. Parr the celebrated, if eccentric, Whig divine to Mackintosh the Scottish lawyer of *Edinburgh Review* fame. The Scot had referred to Coigley and O'Connor as traitors, but Dr. Parr conveyed some hints directed at Mackintosh's own career. " Yes Jamie " said Dr. Parr " he (Coigley) was a bad man but he might have been worse ; he was an Irishman but he might have been a Scotsman, he was a priest but he might have been a lawyer, he was a republican (i.e. traitor) but he might have been an apostate."

twenty one

I

LORD Edward was removed from the Castle to Newgate and given a room overlooking the courtyard to the front. As he contemplated the situation his sufferings were intense. Firstly his health was low, he was not yet recovered from the terrible struggle at the arrest and there was an open and festering wound in his shoulder. The ball had not been extracted and the pain was ceaseless night and day. But these physical wounds were as nothing compared with his mental agony. To one accustomed to travel and excitement, or the alternative of pleasant domesticity, this stagnation was unbearable. His helplessness too had all the intensity of frustration. He was so near the goal. If only he were at liberty for another five days he would have been at the head of his United Irishmen leading them in the attack on Dublin city itself. His mind then ran on the plight of his unfortunate battalions, now almost leaderless and with but vague hope of assistance from the French. When he thought of those brave men his emotion was so great that sometimes his fellow-prisoners heard him cry out in agony in the night.

His physical condition became steadily lower ; the wound had not appeared dangerous but there seemed to be no healing capacity in his general condition. His

mental torture continued ; when not thinking of the
Leinster insurgents his mind ran on his friends, his wife
and children, and not least his dearly-loved mother.
He was now isolated from the world and he did not know
what was happening, for the authorities allowed no
communication whatever with the State Prisoners. It
was explained that as the date for the insurrection was
fixed it was essential to isolate the leaders and it was decided to make no exceptions even in cases of extreme
hardship. So when Lord Edward made his will leaving
all his property to his wife and children the lawyer perforce
had to take his instructions through an intermediary jailer.

The accumulation of suffering brought grave mental
trouble, his mind began to wander, his eyes rolled, his
face became distorted and he roared commands to his
legions. His shouts were heard all over the prison and the
jailers rushed in to hold him down on the bed. In this
state he lingered for about a fortnight, the wound still
festering from the pistol-ball lodged within, while the
infection spread through the whole blood-stream. Then
on the 1st June he got the news that Ryan, whom he had
wounded at the time of his arrest, had died of his wounds.
This brought a turn for the worse, he was now delirious
and his fits alternated with complete exhaustion. He
recovered somewhat and next day he heard a hammering
in the courtyard not far from his cell window. He asked
what the noise was and was told that it was workmen
erecting a gallows. That day a man named Clinch—a
United Irishman—was hanged almost within sight of his cell,
and according to the barbarous custom of the period, the
body was left shuddering in mid-air for almost half an hour.
This was the end ; by that evening Lord Edward was a
gibbering maniac, roaring and gesticulating, attempting
to rise from his bed and falling back exhausted. He
looked so dangerous that two keepers were obtained from
a nearby madhouse who remained with him all night.

II

News travelled slowly in those days and it was not until four days after the arrest—on the 23rd May—that the friends in London first heard of the matter. The Home Secretary himself, the Duke of Portland, a family friend, was the informant. Of recent weeks the family anxiety had been so great that this new disaster could scarcely be said to increase it. But individual reactions were different. The Duchess his mother, already worn out with worry, determined at once to make the journey to Ireland, but was dissuaded when they pointed out that her presence in London, for the moment at all events, was more useful. As an additional precaution the news that Lord Edward was wounded was kept from her for some days as her children really feared that the shock might kill her. The well-loved brother Lord Henry set off for Dublin on the 27th of May. Lucy entreated to be taken with him—both Arthur and Eddy were now in prison there—but the family would not hear of it. The country, it was emphasised, particularly by Ogilvie, was in a state of civil war, and they might all be murdered. With tears in her eyes Lucy begged Henry again to take her, but in vain ; all she could obtain was his promise to send immediate news. If need be, it was agreed that Lucy and the Duchess should leave instantly for Dublin. On this understanding Henry set out.

There is one thing to be said in favour of Lucy's desire to accompany Henry. Her favourite brother was in peril and she alone adverted to the danger from his wound, until as the days passed her constant anxiety increased to the point of hysteria. It may seem odd that the rest of them hardly troubled about this matter of the wound at all, but for this they are scarcely to be blamed, since there was something like a conspiracy among the

surgeons to keep everyone assured that the wound was
not dangerous. The injury in itself may not have been
grave, but Edward's health was low and his mental
suffering and isolation had reduced his resistance to
infection so far that his debility became in itself dangerous.
One would expect that the surgeons had noticed this
complication earlier than two days before the prisoner's
death, but if they did, the family certainly was not told.

For the moment then, the friends in Dublin and London.
concentrated on what seems to us now a relatively unimportant matter—the postponement of the trial. It was
known that the Government proposed to set up a special
Commission to try the State Prisoners, and that Lord
Edward's name was the first on the list, the trial in fact
being fixed for June 11th. Subsequently when the Commission commenced to function this distinction was
accorded to John McCann who was Secretary of the
meeting in Oliver Bond's house. He was tried and condemned together with Bond and young Michael Byrne
and all three were sentenced to the gallows. The two
Sheares had already been executed. The authorities
were ready to embark on a scheme of hanging the State
Prisoners *seriatim*, but as they had upwards of a hundred
in Newgate this horrifying programme was too unnerving
even for the experienced coercionists at the Castle. Overtures were made by some more humane loyalists, and a
compromise was arranged, whereby the remaining State
Prisoners were spared their lives on condition of disclosures
and exile. The compromise arrived just in time to save
Bond, but McCann and Byrne were hanged. Various
kinds of amnesties were proclaimed in the provinces, but
subject to so many exceptions that hundreds were in fact
executed. If Lord Edward had survived he might have
been included in the compromise with the State
Prisoners, (one of whom incidentally was his friend
Arthur O'Connor) unless he had the ill-luck of McCann

and Byrne, in being amongst the first to be condemned and executed before the negotiations were in motion.

The charge against Lord Edward at the least would have been High Treason, and to this there would be added the charge of the murder of Capt. Ryan. There was such an accumulation of evidence against Lord Edward, including those documents in his own handwriting that the death penalty could not have been avoided. At the moment there was a great outcry from an influential section of loyalists for summary punishment of the rebel leaders and the Government was in no mood to resist this demand. There was some purpose therefore in the family attempt to have the trial postponed. It must be remembered that the insurrection was now in progress and in one area at least—Wexford—it was to prove a long and difficult campaign with atrocities on both sides. There was a great feeling of panic in Dublin and elsewhere and this clearly was not the best atmosphere for a trial. If the matter were postponed it might yet be possible to save Lord Edward. Most of all it was necessary to have time for friends in high places to get busy.

It is an indication of the family influence that they had access on Lord Edward's behalf to the King himself. Ogilvie had already written to Richmond but received a polite and cold reply. When Lord Henry wrote later in stronger terms Richmond agreed to mention the matter to William Pitt, suggesting however—rather significantly—that he did not think that postponement would make any material difference. Meanwhile the indefagitable Ogilvie at the request of the Duchess had been aiming at an even higher target. He sent a message to no less a person than the Prince of Wales and received a long and sincere reply in which the Prince promised to do what he could, and authorised Ogilvie to convey to Lord Chancellor Clare that the Prince would be pleased if the trial could be postponed. This was indeed encouraging—but the

King's second son, the Duke of York, went even further. He was a good friend of Lord Edward since the old days in Devonshire House and regretted rather than disapproved the course that Lord Edward had adopted. York said he would speak to the King himself, and this he did without delay and got an unofficial undertaking that the trial would be postponed.

This solicitude throws light on the attitude of the ruling-class in England to Irish affairs. That much maligned man the Prince of Wales, afterwards Regent and George IV, was—so far as one can judge—a sincere friend of the popular cause in Ireland. He had decided to accept the Irish regency in earlier days at the risk even of separating the monarchy but he believed that he was doing it, not merely to get his own back on the Tories, but also to get rid of the corrupt ruling clique in the Castle. As late as 1798 the Castle received the alarming information that the Prince of Wales was involved in some sort of Opposition plan to have the Prince appointed as Lord Lieutenant, and it was understood he would inaugurate a popular regime on democratic principles in Ireland. This report came by a roundabout route from Paris where it was said to be included in a memorandum furnished by Lewins, the Irish agent, to the French authorities. It may be argued that the Prince's partiality towards the Irish opposition arose from dislike of Pitt and his followers, but there is evidence also that his feelings, then and afterwards, were quite genuine.

Another active friend at this tragic time was, as might have been expected, Charles James Fox. He went so far as to offer to accompany Henry to Dublin. Henry arrived in Dublin at the end of May but by then the news trickling out from the prison was extremely serious. Lady Louisa, the aunt, had not ceased to importune the authorities for permission to visit the prisoner, and Henry immediately on arrival took up the struggle, but once again Lord

Clare wrote reiterating all the old arguments and refusing permission. His letter is dated June 3rd and Lord Edward was then dying. In justice to Camden the Lord Lieutenant, Castlereagh the Secretary, and Clare himself, it is possible that they did not realise that the danger to Lord Edward was so great. Henry in his anxiety was driven to desperation. On June 3rd he received a letter smuggled out from a fellow-prisoner which stated that Lord Edward was dangerously ill. " In fact " the letter stated " he is dying, he was delirious some time last night." In this extremity Lady Louisa Conolly, after a fruitless visit to Camden the Lord Lieutenant, again presented herself at the house of Chancellor Clare in Ely Place, and with wild tears begged for his authority that she and Henry might visit the dying man. Clare was in a difficulty. He was a hardened man but he was moved by these pathetic entreaties, and it is said that, despite his evil reputation, he was not altogether an unkindly man. He was aware that, strictly speaking, only the Lord Lieutenant or the Chief Secretary could give the necessary permit. He pointed this out to Lady Louisa, but added that he saw a way out, namely that he himself would conduct them to the prison and to the very cell of the prisoner. There was no time to lose. A chaise was called, the two got in, accompanied by Emily Napier niece of Lady Louisa, and after stopping at Leinster House for Henry, the oddly-assorted party hastened in the summer dusk to the prison.

III

All doors were open to the Chancellor, and soon the aunt and the well-loved brother were in the room where Lord Edward lay, while the Chancellor waited patiently in an adjoining apartment. The prisoner was quiet and pale, with drawn features and half-glazed eyes, occasionally muttering to himself ,but for the most part lying in a semi-swoon of exhaustion. Lady Louisa gave one glance at him and stifled a cry; for with a woman's quick observation she noticed the fixed stare in those glassy eyes and the pallor of death already spreading on those kindly and noble features.

For three weeks Lord Edward had not seen or heard from his friends. Now after the violent agitation occasioned by the death of Ryan and the hanging of Clinch, he was too exhausted to show any surprise. Stifling her emotion Lady Louisa approached the bed, Lord Edward looked at her vaguely for a moment, he recognised her and kissed her, murmuring " It is heaven to see you! " As yet Henry kept in the background fearing that his brother was too worn out to withstand any further emotional strain.

Lord Edward lay quietly and smiled at his aunt affectionately, though it was evident that his mind was wandering. He did not speak much being unable to form consecutive sentences. In pain from his wound, he turned away from her but his next words were " I can't see you " and Lady Louisa then went round to the other side of the bed. It consoled and soothed him to be able to fix his dim eyes on her face, again he kissed her hand and gave her that sweet child-like smile which she knew so well.

Perceiving now that he was sufficiently recovered from what she feared might be the shock of their coming, Lady Louisa decided that it was time for Lord Henry to come forward. She said simply " Henry has come ". Lord Edward took the news calmly at first as if a matter of course, but in a moment his joy was so great that it agitated him and he asked excitedly " Where is the dear fellow? " Henry quickly came forward to the bed and the two brothers embraced again and again, saying no words, shedding no tears, all their lifelong affection evident in their silence under the shadow of death. Lady Louisa was so overcome at the sight that, drawing apart, her tears fell freely; she was faint but by an effort regained her composure. Lord Edward enquired feelingly for his wife and children and being assured of their safety he relapsed into silence again. It is not recorded that he made any enquiries for other members of his family, but doubtless he was reassured about them in the course of the fitful conversation. He seemed content to rest passively in the proximity of his brother.

But now the time had come for the visitors to go, they had been with him almost an hour and his exhaustion was great. Presently however he became more agitated. Confused recollections of the United Irishmen came to his mind, he was obsessed with the responsibility of leading these poor untrained rebels against the organised military. Lady Louisa appealed to him not to worry about these matters just now and he promised that he would try to put them out of his mind. She and Henry rose to leave asking him to compose himself and promising to return in the morning. He seemed glad of this and the two withdrew.

But the desolation and silence, where for awhile there had been a semblance of normality, caused a frightful reaction. The images driven away by the tranquil presences of Lady Louisa and Henry crowded in upon the prisoner to renew his terror. With the heightened sensibility which often comes with approaching death he confused past and present in a torment of recollection. And there was now no kindly hand or voice to soothe him but a loneliness more bitter and more terrible because for awhile it had been dispelled. There was no one to hear his frenzied cries save the jailer whose laconic account says only that ' a struggle took place ' which commenced soon after the departure of Lord Henry and Lady Louisa and lasted two hours. It was his death agony. He was so young, only thirty-five ; to die was to leave so much— wife, children, family,—and the great adventure of living. But there was no strength left in his exhausted frame to counter this last attack, and sometime in the early hours of June 4th Lord Edward breathed his last.

The following night he was buried secretly by prison officials in a vault in the churchyard of St. Werburgh. He who would have fallen so gallantly amid the excitement and panoply of battle had met his death in the squalor of a prison-cell comforted only by a prison-warder. The cortege of him who was the most illustrious of the Geraldine race, the hero of his people, wended its way with furtive tread through deserted midnight streets watched only by hushed pickets of Orangemen. No friends were there, and in the half-light of the summer night the small group went by with muffled tread. The sound of footsteps died away and then—there was silence once more.

Epilogue

§ 1.

The criminal law of the period required that a man convicted of treason and certain other offences suffered not only in his person, but that his property be forfeited to the Crown. In the case of Lord Edward Fitzgerald there was no conviction by a court of law, and the authorities decided therefore to proceed by way of a Bill of Attainder in Parliament. A Bill was introduced by Toler, the Attorney General, in July 1798. The procedure differed somewhat from the process of ordinary legislation and was a relic of the ancient judicial functions of Parliament. Witnesses were examined before the House and evidence was given of the activities of Lord Edward and the two others named in the Bill, Bagenal Harvey and Cornelius Grogan. The principal witness was Thomas Reynolds. The Bill quickly passed through both Houses and was forwarded for the Royal Assent in September.

Even at this stage the friends of Lord Edward did not despair. A lengthy petition was drafted and presented to the Sovereign, praying for the refusal of the Assent. This was a forlorn hope, as the King's Assent is a formality, but the text of the petition is useful now as detailing the harsh nature of the proceedings. It was signed by Richmond, Ogilvie, Lord Henry Fitzgerald, Charles James Fox, and Lord Holland. Some good may have derived from the petition, however, as the Government decided to allow the estate to be sold in Chancery, and it was bought in by Ogilvie for £10,500. It was settled on the eldest son of Lord Edward, Edward Fox Fitzgerald, then aged five, with charges in favour of the two daughters, Lucy and the younger Pamela; nothing is said about Pamela the widow.

Apart from the forfeiture of property the precise effect, if any, in modern times of " attaint of the blood " is not evident; it did not interfere with the military career or preferment of Lord Edward's son. Nonetheless the family never relaxed efforts to have the Act repealed by the Union Parliament in Westminster. They had the ardent support of at least two Royal Dukes (the Duke of York was an old friend of Lord Edward), and of the Whigs in general by virtue of the Fox connection. The Prince Regent, though he had forsaken the Whigs in 1813 had not forgotten his former enthusiasms and was favourably disposed. The Bill was introduced in 1819 by Lord Liverpool, the Prime Minister, and the Act of Attainder was quickly repealed.

§ 2.

There may be some curiosity about the subsequent fate of Pamela, especially as no provision appears to have been made for her in the settlement on the children. When Lord Edward was " on the run " she stayed with friends in Upper Merrion Street, near Leinster House, and on the evening of his arrest she was attending a ball in the house of Lord Moira on the quays. After the arrest of Lord Edward an Order was made by the Lord Lieutenant, under emergency powers, banishing her from the Kingdom. She was just bereaved of her husband, she had a baby two months old, and she was charged with no crime; yet the Lord Lieutenant, Camden, saw fit to make the Order, which must seem to us especially harsh. She went accordingly to Goodwood, the home of the Duke of Richmond; her eldest son Edward was already there with his grandmother the Duchess Emily, and she took with her the baby Lucy and her daughter Pamela aged three.

It has been suggested the Fitzgeralds treated her rather coolly. They were the " good family "; they had affection for Pamela because she was the wife of the beloved Eddy. Now, however, she was a widow. It is fair to say that these allegations are not borne out by the evidence. Pamela was penniless, and the first step was to deal with that situation. The Fitzgeralds between them made up sufficient money to tide over immediate wants, and it was then decided that further decisions be postponed pending the outcome of the Attainder proceedings. Lady Sarah Napier, Lord Edward's aunt, took a particular interest and showed great consideration, although it was the other aunt, Lady Louisa Conolly, who looked on Lord Edward as her favourite nephew. The Duchess Emily was making the case that they could not do very much financially, because, as she put it, " We are all so poor now." Perhaps there was some truth in this, but if so we are obliged to reckon by ducal standards of the time. A large part of the province of Leinster was devastated in the rebellion, and the Duke of Leinster's income, it was said, had dropped from £30,000 to £20,000 a year. But there was plenty of money in the family nevertheless.

Very soon the result of the Attainder was known, and in the meantime a further complication had developed in Goodwood. The Duke of Richmond, as befitted a great-grandson of Charles II, had always taken a generous interest in the ladies. He was now a fairly vigorous man in his early sixties, a widower of three years' standing, and it was natural that he should look with favour on the beautiful and tragic widow of twenty-four. The rumour went round that he wished to make her his wife. Nothing came of it in the event, perhaps Richmond was restrained by the presence of his formidable sister, the Duchess Emily; possibly the widow Pamela herself did not favour him. A short time previously the Duchess of Leinster had been writing lovingly from Goodwood about Pamela to her son Lord Henry. " There is no need to hurry, she is welcome, I'm sure, to stay here as long as she likes; my brother Richmond is extremely fond of her and enters into her situation with Paternal Solicitude ". Very soon, however, she piped a different note. She wrote to her daughter Lady Sophia, " Indeed, my dear Sophia, it was better she went away. I could give you many Reasons that you would think Good ". Alas for our curiosity, she does not disclose any of those good reasons. All we can say is that they cannot have been financial reasons. As stated Ogilvie arranged to buy in the estate and settle it on the children, surely then the first charge would have been in favour of the widow.

The Fitzgeralds afterwards strongly denied the rumours that Richmond had wished to marry her. There is not much evidence one way or the other. If Richmond had desired to take Pamela as wife, there was nothing to prevent him. There is a letter of his to his sister the Duchess Emily dated 17th June 1798, in which he is non-committal; he refers to Pamela as " a most interesting Object ". This, however, was written before the sojourn of Pamela at Goodwood. There is unfortunately nothing else to show the real state of the Duke's feelings. Soon afterwards Pamela, when she had departed to the Continent, wrote to Lucy from Hamburg: "I'm truly grateful to the Duke of Richmond for his kindness and am sure it was for my good and for my children ". The latter remark hardly seems necessary unless reference is made to something more than normal hospitality. It may well be that Pamela was the unwilling party; there were three children it is true, but she was an extremely attractive young woman. She may have felt there would be no lack of suitors, and the guess proved correct. We may conclude by saying that there must have been some grounds for the Richmond story. Many years afterwards, Madame Ducrest, the great friend and confidant of Pamela, stated positively that Richmond had offered marriage; and it must be presumed that Pamela herself had repeated this to her confidant.

§ 3.

It appears that Pamela's absence from England was intended to be temporary. She took her daughter Pamela with her, but it is difficult to understand that a mother would have left behind an infant of a few months old and also her son Edward. Hamburg was selected as a temporary refuge and some reasons were given for the choice. It was stated that money was coming to her there from the estate of a relative. The city was the nominal home of Madame de Genlis, now banished from France, though at the moment Madame was living in Berlin. She sent Pamela an invitation to come to that city but received a curt refusal, and she records in her journal that " I was very much upset indeed ". The chief attraction of Hamburg, however, was the fact that her girlhood friend Hariette de Sercey, niece of Madame de Genlis was now living there, married to a wealthy banker named Mathiessen; as was a daughter of Madame de Genlis, also a former *élève*, married to General Count Valence.

She continued to correspond with the Fitzgeralds chiefly in connection with the two children, and also as to the possibility of obtaining money from the estate for the maintenance and education of the younger Pamela. She repeatedly pointed out that Pamela was the daughter of Lord Edward and that the Fitzgerald estate should provide for the upbringing. Gradually the letters became less frequent. Then rumours came that Pamela was to marry again. Lady Sarah Napier wrote from Ireland telling of a conversation with Sir John Crawford, a Government official who had been in Hamburg. He may be presumed to be a reliable witness, for Lady Sarah describes him as a " dull matter-of-fact honest Man ". Crawford, it appears, had moved in the same circles as Pamela in Hamburg, and said that she was leading a quiet and eminently respectable life, living *en pension* in the Mathiessen household, and that she had many admirers. He mentioned two in particular, a Colonel Harcourt, of whom we hear no more, and Mr. Pitcairn, the United States Consul-General. Lady Sarah enquired of Crawford as to the rumours of marriage. She wanted to make clear that so far as the Fitzgeralds were concerned they did not object; all that worried them was the fear that Pamela would not find someone good enough for her.

A year or so later Pamela married the Consul-General Mr. Pitcairn. It is not on record that the family considered him " not good enough ", but they certainly acted as if they did. Almost all communication ceased after the marriage, and no money was sent for the maintenance of Lord Edward's child Pamela. This embittered Pamela exceedingly, and had a permanent effect. She remained for many years in communication with her sister-in-law Lady Sophia (with whom her daughter Lucy lived), but all the others had ceased to answer her letters. Even Lady Lucy, now married, the bosom friend of the happy days in Kildare Lodge, had ceased to write.

§ 4.

For the next ten or twelve years, Pamela is a shadowy figure, though her name comes up occasionally in a fleeting entry in the reminiscences of the time. Otherwise her life and movements are unknown. We cannot even say if the marriage with Pitcairn was happy or not; it endured until 1812 and there was one child, a daughter. In that year Mr. Pitcairn left for the United States, taking with him his daughter, and he and Pamela did not meet again. The chance references made to him describe him as a respectable and kindly man, yet somehow he sounds dull. There was no deep estrangement and no formal separation; almost twenty years later, on being informed of the death of his wife Pamela, Pitcairn wrote from America with great feeling and offered to pay all the expenses of her funeral.

The question arises whether Pamela ever revisited England or Ireland, or saw her children again. In this connection Madame de Genlis tells an extraordinary story. The date is uncertain, but as Madame was allowed by the Emperor to return to Paris in 1804 the episode may be placed as taking place shortly after that date.

Madame de Genlis had a *protégé* named Casimir, who was returning to Paris from London in the suite of Prince Esterhazy, a Hungarian nobleman. While waiting to go on board the Prince's yacht, Casimir came across Pamela distressed and alone in a Dover boarding-house. Her story was that she had " fled from creditors in London to avoid arrest ". She was trying to make her way to France but was afraid to go out of doors on account of the bailiffs; if they found her, she said, they would take her back to London under arrest. She had no money, could Casimir lend her the equivalent of £50 and smuggle her on board the yacht? Otherwise she would surely be caught. The astonished Casimir did all that was required, and Pamela reached Paris in safety. It is not surprising that she got a chilly welcome from Madame de Genlis who ordered her to go back at once to her husband, Pitcairn, and her two daughters (one Pitcairn's child) in Hamburg.

Though Madame de Genlis is unreliable, it would be unreasonable to suppose that she could have imagined this episode. On the other hand, it offends against probability that a lady in Pamela's plight, abandoned and alone in a strange country, a fugitive in a Dover boarding-house, should suddenly have run across a friend with money and a private yacht. We may assume, however, that she did visit London, and that she stayed a considerable time, as otherwise she could not have accumulated debts. Yet the Fitzgeralds, voluminous correspondents and diarists as they were, never even mention this visit, which would surely have been a matter of great family interest. Even Sophia, who had sincere affection for Pamela and in whose care the baby Lucy had been left, does not mention it.

What was the purpose of the trip to England, if indeed it took place at all? Two answers are suggested. As a mother, she wished to see her children and arrange for their future, secondly she was endeavouring to obtain an allowance by way of dower. In this latter quest she failed. Legally her right of dower was extinguished when the estate was forfeited, and according to Madame Ducrest, Pamela received nothing after her marriage to Pitcairn. The question of an allowance from the Fitzgerald estate was not pressed while the Pitcairn marriage endured, that is to say, until 1812. Pamela repeatedly pointed out that it was unfair that Pitcairn should maintain and educate Lord Edward's daughter Pamela. The Fitzgeralds refused to provide for her, though they offered to take her and have her educated in England.

Pamela eventually agreed to this course, when her daughter was aged about twelve or thirteen. Afterwards Pamela received a substantial yearly allowance from the Orleans family, and when her son Edward Fox Fitzgerald came into his heritage in 1815 he supplemented this with a payment of £200 a year. What is not explained is how she should have accumulated debts in London and who would have given her credit. She had a certain reputation for extravagance, and we must presume that she convinced people that she had rights against the Fitzgerald estate.

Pamela inspired affection in many people; as is evident from the letters of Emily Duchess of Leinster and her acquaintances. Though she was often self-willed and wayward she appears on the whole to have been pliable and somewhat colourless. The abandonment of her children is a matter which, to say the least of it, must cause surprise. She justified it by saying that she sent her children to the Fitzgeralds in England to be educated and brought up in suitable environment. This sounds plausible, but it does not explain the handing over of her first-born infant, Edward, to his grandmother the Duchess when he was only a few months old, thereafter seeing little of him again; or why she left the infant Lucy behind, or why she allowed Pitcairn to take her daughter to America, knowing perhaps that she would never see her again. After that, in 1814, or thereabouts, she was entirely alone, but the following year, after a stay in Vienna, she made a new and important acquaintance.

He was Louis Laval, Duc de la Force, a soldier of some distinction. Pamela was then nearly forty, and though the tradition survived that she was a coquette, and that she sought and enjoyed admiration, her beauty was departed. She appears to have suffered from some glandular disease which made her very portly. As for de la Force, he had an in-and-out career. Originally an *émigré*, he afterwards served in the Napoleonic armies

s

and figured in the retreat from Moscow. After Waterloo
he sided with the Bourbons, and adhered to them during
the Hundred Days. He was imprisoned for a time, but
on the Restoration he was given a military command in
the south of France and lived in his chateau at Montaubon
near Toulouse. Pamela had been living in Paris in 1816
and 1817. She joined de la Force at Montaubon and
lived there for the rest of her life, but whether in the
chateau or in her own cottage nearby is uncertain. They
were both past middle-age and their association endured
until Pamela's death in 1831. Dr. Madden visited her
at Montaubon in 1820, but all he says is " I saw Pamela
at Toulouse, where she was then living (having resumed
the name of Fitzgerald) apart from her second husband ".
Here he stops abruptly. Madden was a well-meaning but
rather censorious individual, and he had a charitable
way of side-tracking the awkward interludes. Also he
had strong likes and dislikes. It is annoying that on
this occasion he did not tell us more: what conversation
did they have, what had Pamela to say for herself, what
precisely was her relationship with de la Force? Instead
of dealing with this, he is merely at great pains to refute
charges of eccentricity brought against Pamela: that,
for instance, she always dressed in the costume of a
shepherdess. The tradition that lingered in the district
was that Pamela was a kindly and well-loved lady who
did much good work amongst the poor.

§ 5.

In the autumn of 1831 Pamela and the Duc de la
Force went on a visit to Paris and put up in the Hotel
du Danube in the Rue Richepanse. Pamela was taken
seriously ill and was visited immediately by her old
friend and companion Madame Ducrest niece of Madame
de Genlis, who showed great kindness and was in constant

attendance as a nurse. She lingered several weeks and died peacefully in November 1831. The only member of the Fitzgerald family who called was the Comtesse de Chabot, formerly Lady Charlotte Fitzgerald, daughter of William (the second Duke) and niece of Lord Edward. This lady resided in Paris and, according to Madame Ducrest, she was not on good terms with Pamela, but when the end was approaching she came in response to a request on a long and friendly visit. She came again on subsequent days.

Pamela's death was peaceful but rather friendless and lonely, the only persons present being Madame Ducrest and a nurse. The Duc de la Force, her companion for over fifteen years, though he sincerely lamented her passing, seems to have been frightened off at this stage; the priest who attended Pamela advised that the Duc should leave the Hotel. An unedifying state of affairs developed after the death. Madame Ducrest discovered that Pamela had no money, not even sufficient to pay the funeral-expenses; as the matter was of great urgency she got in touch with the Fitzgerald connections in Paris; they however would do nothing and refused even to attend the funeral. In desperation, Madame Ducrest sent a message to the Orleans family, and the Princess Adelaide, half-sister of Pamela, immediately took the affair in hand. She was buried in Montmartre, and a headstone with the following inscription was placed over the grave (the " L.L." is for Louis Laval Duc de la Force):

A. Pamela

Lady Edward Fitzgerald

Par

Son Ami Le Plus Dévoué

L. L.

Thirty years later the remains were removed to England and interred in the Fitzgerald family plot at Thames Ditton in Surrey.

APPENDIX I

Chronology

1747 Marriage of James Earl of Kildare with Lady Emily Lennox.

1763 Birth of Lord Edward Fitzgerald.

1773 Death of James 1st Duke of Leinster.

1774 The Duchess and family go to France.

1774 Marriage of Duchess of Leinster with William Ogilvie.

1779 Lord Edward joins the Sussex militia.

1780 Goes to Ireland as lieutenant in the 96th.

1781 Lord Edward serves in America.

1783 In St. Lucia.

1783 Returns to Ireland. Enters Parliament.

1786 Goes to Woolwich, makes tour of Channel Island.

1787 Attends session of Irish Parliament.
     Makes tour in Spain.

1788 Joins the 54th in Nova Scotia.

1788 The Regency debates in the Irish Parliament.

1790 Returns to Ireland.

1791 Attends session of Irish Parliament.

1792 In London; friendship with Paine and others.
     Goes to Paris.

1792 Name removed from Army list. Meets Madame de Genlis
     and Pamela.

1792 (December) Marriage of Pamela with Lord Edward Fitz-
     gerald.

1793 Returns to Dublin. Lives in " Frescati ".

1794 Settles in Kildare Lodge.

1795 Meets Arthur O'Connor. Recall of Lord Fitzwilliam.

1796 Lord Edward and Arthur O'Connor admitted to the United Irishmen.

1796 Fitzgerald and O'Connor confer with French delegates in Hamburg and Switzerland.

1796 (December) French Fleet at Bantry Bay.

1797 Address to the people of Kildare. Appointed Commander-in-Chief of forces of the United Irishmen.

1798 12th March. Arrest of the Leinster Directory at Oliver Bond's house.

    30th March. Martial Law proclaimed.

    19th May. Arrest of Lord Edward.

    4th June. Death of LORD EDWARD FITZGERALD.

1800 Marriage of Pamela with Mr. Pitcairn at Hamburg.

1805 (?) Pamela returns on visit to London from Hamburg.

1812 Pamela and Pitcairn separate.

1813-14 Pamela in Vienna.

1815 Pamela settles in Montaubon.

1831 Death of Pamela.

APPENDIX II

(From *Falkener's Journal*, July 27, 1797.)

Lord Edward Fitzgerald's Address to the Electors of the County Kildare.

"I take this opportunity of thanking my fellow-citizens for the favour they conferred on me at the last general election. I hope the conduct I pursued since met their approbation; it was dictated by the purest motives and most fervent wish for the welfare and happiness of Ireland. I shall not offer myself at present a candidate, feeling that, under the present circumstances, there can be no free election in Ireland; any return made will be only by sufferance of the nearest military commanding officer. What is to be expected from a parliament returned under martial law? Looking to the true spirit of the British constitution, I doubt if a body elected under such circumstances, can be called a parliament, or its acts reckoned binding.

"I hope my fellow-citizens of the county of Kildare will not look on my declining to stand a candidate now as abandoning their interests. I trust to see the day when I shall offer myself to represent them in a parliament that will be freely and fairly elected, and can be venerated by all honest men.

"Though not your representative, believe me always your faithful servant,

"EDWARD FITZGERALD.

"Kildare, July 14th, 1797."

APPENDIX III

Table showing descent of Lord Edward Fitzgerald on the maternal side.

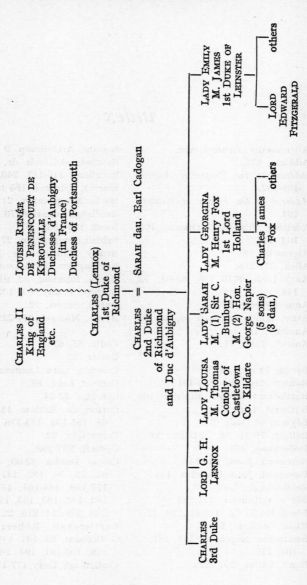

CHARLES II = LOUISE RENÉE
King of   DE PENENCOUET DE
England   KÉROUALLE
etc.   Duchesse d'Aubigny
               (in France)
               Duchess of Portsmouth

CHARLES (Lennox)
1st Duke of
Richmond

CHARLES = SARAH dau. Earl Cadogan
2nd Duke
of Richmond
and Duc d'Aubigny

CHARLES | LORD G. H. | LADY LOUISA | LADY SARAH | LADY GEORGINA | LADY EMILY
3rd Duke | LENNOX | M. Thomas | M. (1) Sir C. | M. Henry Fox | M. JAMES
 | | Conolly of | Bunbury | 1st Lord | 1st DUKE OF
 | | Castletown | M. (2) Hon. | Holland | LEINSTER
 | | Co. Kildare | George Napier | |
 | | | (5 sons) | Charles James | LORD
 | | | (3 dau.) | Fox | EDWARD
 | | | | others | FITZGERALD
 | | | | | others

index

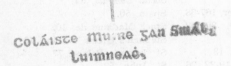